MIKHAIL BARYSHNIKOV

GENIUS!
The Artist and the Process

MIKHAIL BARYSHNIKOV

by

Bruce Glassman

SILVER BURDETT PRESS

Created and produced by: Blackbirch Graphics, Inc.

Project Editor: Emily Easton
Designer: Cynthia Minichino
Cover Design: Leslie Bauman

Manufactured in The United States of America

10 9 8 7 6 5 4 3 2 1

Library of Congress Cataloging-in-Publication Data

Glassman, Bruce.
  Mikhail Baryshnikov / by Bruce Glassman.
  (Genius!: the artist and the process)
  Includes bibliographical references.
  Summary: A biography of the brilliant ballet dancer who went on to become a choreographer, film actor, and director of the American Ballet Theatre.
  1. Baryshnikov, Mikhail, 1948 — Juvenile literature.   2. Ballet dancers — Biography — Juvenile literature.   [1. Baryshnikov, Mikhail, 1948-   .   2. Ballet dancers.]   I. Title.   II. Series: Genius! (Englewood Cliffs, N.J.)   GV1785.B348G58   1990   92—dc20 [792.8'092] [B]
ISBN 0-382-09907-9 (lib. bdg.)   90-34335
ISBN 0-382-24035-9 (hard)   CIP
                                        AC

(Frontispiece)
After proving himself in the world of ballet, Baryshnikov achieved stardom in the United States on Broadway and in films.

Contents

There's a moment when you witness the magic of the theater, and you're hooked. There's no way back.
—Mikhail Baryshnikov

CHAPTER 1

THE DREAM TO DANCE

The scene is the Kirov Ballet in Leningrad, USSR, 1966. Pregraduate students from the prestigious Vaganova school are performing *Le Corsaire* on the Kirov stage for the highest ranking ballet officials in the country. The word is out about a young dancer who has shown exceptional promise, and comparisons to the great Rudolf Nureyev are already being exchanged between insiders.

The young man takes the stage and debuts with an incredible combination of steps—performing seemingly without effort. The crowd is awed by his grand *pirouette*—perfectly executed with incomparable majesty. Thunderous applause and cries of "Bravo!" after the performance punctuate the beginning of a career that starts out brilliantly and only improves.

The young dancer was Mikhail Baryshnikov, known to his friends as "Misha." His debut on the Kirov stage—the same stage on which he would dance for eight more years—marked Baryshnikov's entry into the elite world of Soviet ballet. His success that evening came as no surprise to most teachers and dancers in the Soviet ballet community. Word of Baryshnikov's unique talent had been spreading quickly ever since his first day at the Vaganova school. Everyone who saw him dance spotted it immediately: he had something special. His body was nearly perfectly formed. His precision in executing dance combinations was unfailing. His technique was astonishing.

Baryshnikov's performance in *Le Corsaire* was the beginning of a career that would propel him beyond his wildest imagination. It would be his consuming passion for dance that would cause him to abandon his native land and leave his past behind him.

Born on January 27, 1948, in the Latvian capital of Riga (northwestern Russia), Misha knew few happy times at home. His mother, Alexandra Kiseleva, was a seamstress and the second wife to his father, high-ranking Soviet officer Nikolai Baryshnikov. Each partner brought to their union a child from a previous marriage. Alexandra had a son and Nikolai had a daughter. Misha's half-brother was nine when he was born, and the two of them spent a good deal of time together as children. Their half-sister, who was considerably older, lived in Leningrad.

Unfortunately, Alexandra and Nikolai's second marriage offered little lasting happiness to either partner. Baryshnikov remembers his father as a very difficult man: "There was no rapport between my mother, half-brother, and him—no great sense of love and trust. It was not a very happy family. I felt the

Riga, Latvia, 1948, the birthplace of Mikhail Baryshnikov.

tension from very early on. My mother was actually never very happy with my father. He was extremely impulsive, very nervous, and highly neurotic."

Nikolai came from a well-off industrialist family (his father and grandfather had a factory in the middle of Russia) and was very well educated. His early enrollment into military school during the Stalin era only increased his austere and commanding nature.

Misha's mother, Alexandra, was very different from her husband. Born into a peasant family from a small out-of-the-way village near the Volga River, she was an energetic, ambitious, and individualistic woman who easily grew tired of situations in which she felt constrained. Alexandra loved music, art, the theater, and particularly the ballet. Unfortunately, her love of the arts was not shared by her husband. Often, this difference between them resulted in arguments and tension, only deepening Misha's mother's unhappiness with Nikolai.

The dark side of Alexandra's usual energy and elation was her severe and frequent depression. Though much of this was probably triggered by her unfulfilling marriage, much surely came from deeper, more complex psychological troubles. Her unstable emotional health and her unhappy marriage were more than she could bear, and in 1959, when Misha was only eleven years old, Alexandra committed suicide.

Misha was devastated by his mother's death, although at that time he was unaware that she had taken her own life. The young boy was told that his mother had died of a sudden disease. It would be years before he would overhear a conversation that revealed the truth.

This loss—and his tormented boyhood—had a great impact on the dancer's life as he grew older. His hardships created in him an emotional complexity that enabled him to achieve great expressiveness as an artist. They also remained as a constant source of pain and unhappiness. Baryshnikov recalls his early home life this way: "Nothing dramatic happened every day, but it was not a family unit. That's why I fell very much in love with the theater. It was my escape from family reality."

Even at a tender age, young Mikhail demonstrates the easy grace that would make him famous.

For the young boy, theater and dance were more than just an escape; they were an opportunity to release real emotions under the guise of make-believe. Unable to communicate his unhappiness at home, especially to his father, Baryshnikov hid his pain behind the various masks he wore and the roles he played on the stage.

Shortly before his mother's death, the young Baryshnikov became seriously interested in ballet. Though he had played soccer and other sports at school, he had fallen in love with dance at the age of six, after his mother had taken him to his first ballet. Baryshnikov's father often scoffed at his wife for bringing their son to the ballet. But, on this point, Alexandra never gave in. Five years after his first introduction to ballet, the young Baryshnikov decided to audition at the Riga dance school.

Riga was a large, cosmopolitan city where Russian culture mingled with European culture. The Riga dance school, in particular, had a reputation for excellent training and rigorous entrance requirements. Mikhail's mother, a devoted ballet lover, brought her son to audition for the school. After a thorough examination and audition, young Mikhail was asked to start the program immediately. By 1960, at the age of twelve, Baryshnikov was Riga's newest dance student.

Shortly after Alexandra's death, Nikolai married a woman he had known in his youth. Misha was thirteen when his stepmother moved in. The two of them had an "okay relationship," as the dancer recalls, but not a long one. Two years after his stepmother arrived, Mikhail left for Leningrad to study ballet.

Although dance in Russia had long been considered a noble art, Baryshnikov's father had never approved of Mikhail's love for ballet. In the 1950s, when Mikhail was growing up, many Russians thought ballet to be a frivolous profession suited only to girls. Boys were expected to become engineers, builders, and pilots. The almost instant approval of his instructors at the dance school, however, managed to convince even Nikolai that his son was destined to dance.

The shape of Misha's career was somewhat influenced by changing attitudes toward ballet in the USSR during the 1960s. His formative years as a dancer coincided with the "cultural thaw" during Premier Khrushchev's regime in the USSR, when the country's great cultural heritage experienced a rebirth. Much of its cultural past had been criticized and ignored while Josef Stalin was in power from 1929 to 1953.

The Stalin era was a brutal chapter in Soviet history. Convinced that the USSR should isolate itself from the rest of the world, Stalin created a state in which military might and nationalistic pride were of supreme importance. Stalin's army became a ruthless watchdog of the Soviet people, one that eliminated any hint of opposition to its leader's ideology. Hundreds of thousands of Russian writers, teachers, artists, and other citizens who were suspected of disloyalty to Mother Russia were arrested, imprisoned, or killed without trial or warning during Stalin's "Reign of Terror."

Because fear and censorship ruled the country during this period, the new Soviet generation was skeptical about many of the values and attitudes that predominated in Stalin's era. They seemed to approach life with less optimism than their elders. Conventional careers lost favor and pursuits in the liberal arts became more popular. During this time of changing attitudes, ballet once again became a fashionable outlet for young artists. Unfortunately, budding creative dancers like Baryshnikov soon found out that even though censorship of the arts was somewhat less, political control remained strong in every aspect of Soviet culture. No art was immune to politics, most particularly ballet.

The Soviet ballet has a long history of greatness. Many feel it is the best in the world. Because of its great value to the image of the country, the USSR traditionally kept tight control on its ballet community. Choreographers and directors were constantly pressured to mount productions that would glorify communist ideals. Communist Party leaders and KGB agents watched ballet stars to make sure that the country's prized symbols of perfection did not stray in their loyalties. To this end, the members of the Kirov had to

From 1929 to 1953, the Soviet Union was ruled with an iron hand by dictator Josef Stalin.

regularly attend Party meetings. At those meetings, dancers would be told that their achievements on the stage were first and foremost for the benefit of the USSR, and only second for the purposes of artistic fulfillment.

By 1962, after only two years in the Riga program, Misha was placed in an advanced class normally reserved for dancers who had danced for eight or nine years. Baryshnikov believes much of his success was due to his wonderful relationship with his instructor, Yuris Kapralis, who was also a Latvian. Kapralis immediately recognized in his young student a greatness beyond compare. He inspired Misha to pursue dance and helped to turn the small, muscular body of a little gymnast into a form befitting classical ballet.

Alexander Godunov, renowned dancer and classmate for three years at Riga, recalled that "Misha was a wonderboy whose phenomenal physical equipment [was] combined with extreme zest and conscientiousness." Godunov and Baryshnikov, who were friends in school, spent many hours together, rehearsing and studying. Often, they spent their free time devising silly new ways to grow taller or to increase their muscle power.

By the time he was fifteen, Baryshnikov was invited to join a Riga dance troupe that toured and performed for teenagers. During a stop in Leningrad, he visited the famous Vaganova school of dance and happened upon a class being taught by the great Russian teacher Alexander Pushkin. Not hoping for much, Baryshnikov approached the instructor and said, "I would very much like to be your pupil." Pushkin felt Misha's legs and body and asked him to jump up and down. The young boy then had a quick physical from the school's doctors and was told they would be in touch. He spent that summer awaiting final word. "It would have been shattering if I had not been accepted," Baryshnikov reflected later. He was already thinking nonstop about what life would be like at the Vaganova school.

He dreamed of being a part of Leningrad, the cultural capital of the country and an immense, sprawling, exciting city that seemed to have limitless opportunities. Riga, though cosmopolitan, was more isolated and conventional than Leningrad. He saw Riga as a known quantity, Leningrad as a challenge. "Seeing Leningrad was like an electrifying shock. I could not imagine living apart from it," Baryshnikov recalls thinking after his first visit.

Finally, word of his acceptance arrived, and Baryshnikov left home for the first time. His friend

Godunov was also admitted to the Kirov's Vaganova school in Leningrad, but only Misha was admitted to the elite class of Alexander Pushkin. The two young men would pursue different careers and would not cross paths again until seventeen years later in the United States, when they would work together at the American Ballet Theatre in New York.

Once enrolled, the new pupil quickly realized how demanding the prestigious Vaganova program actually was. Students worked from nine o'clock in the morning to ten o'clock at night. Misha studied fencing; theatrical make-up; French, Russian, and Western literature; as well as dancing. The Vaganova curriculum was famous for its instruction in acting, particularly in mime. Baryshnikov accepted the rigor of the program eagerly. All the demands seemed well worth the opportunity to study with Pushkin. There was something special between teacher and student that energized Misha and compelled him to achieve excellence in all aspects of his art. About his relationship with Pushkin, he says, "Well, he obviously recognized in me some possibilities. He gave me a lot of special attention and worked with me privately. . . . He was a saint and also a very simple person. . . . He liked me."

Living with nine other students in a crowded Vaganova dormitory room, Baryshnikov often found himself a guest at Pushkin's house. The dance teacher was always happy to provide his students with food and an environment for lively discussion. Pushkin cultivated a special bond with Misha—one that had been cultivated only once before, with young Rudolf Nureyev—and became Misha's intellectual mentor as well as his physical one. "I was his last pupil," Baryshnikov remembers. "I will never find the kind of pedagogue I had in Pushkin. He was such a pure and simple character that it is hard to talk about him in

Young Baryshnikov, in 1968, at work in the class of famed dance instructor, Alexander Pushkin.

simple words. He was like somebody who stepped out of an icon. Pushkin had an ability to infect you with such a love for dance that you almost became obsessed with it. It is almost like a disease."

The years with Pushkin would prove to be one of the most extraordinary influences on Baryshnikov's career. Pushkin's style of teaching followed a natural, instinctual form of learning in which the dancer is not given any specific movements but rather is allowed to let the body and the muscles train themselves. This freed the dancer from having to constantly think about every movement.

Great emphasis was placed on toning the muscles since they were the support for every movement. Pushkin was also brilliant at training others to do the *grand jeté* (a long leap forward), for which he had been so famous. Pushkin had learned how to leap from the great Russian dancer Maryinsky. Nureyev got his leap from Pushkin. Baryshnikov's leap, which was naturally high and wide, became even more astounding under Pushkin's guidance. Their hard work began to receive public attention by 1966 when Misha won a gold medal at the Varna International Competition in Bulgaria.

Fortunately, Pushkin's method of teaching fit perfectly with the young Baryshnikov, who already possessed an advanced natural ability and a real yearning to make new discoveries about dance on his own. The technique was most suited for a dancer with intense discipline and an unwavering drive to attain perfection. Misha was, of course, just this kind of dancer. His inner-directedness and clear vision of his goals were the ideal match for the less-controlling and more-exploring style of Pushkin. Baryshnikov explains that "it was as if everything came of itself. But that was Pushkin's strength. . . . Patiently and without pressure, he would bring the student to the idea of self-education. Everyone taught himself under his guidance." Chinko Rafique, a classmate of Baryshnikov's in Pushkin's class, remembers that Misha "was like a sponge, soaking up everything, and [Pushkin] had only to give him the slightest direction."

Misha was placed into the Kirov dance company after only three years of study at Vaganova. This kind of advancement was unheard of. Yet, all of Misha's teachers felt he was so exceptional that this accelerated promotion was only logical. What was even more amazing, however, was the fact that Baryshnikov entered the company as a soloist, passing over the usual required service in the *corps de ballet* (the supporting members of a ballet company who dance as a unit). Of course, his special treatment did not go unnoticed by the other dancers and students. Many of Baryshnikov's jealous colleagues shunned him. Others did not want to dance with him out of spite. Nevertheless, everyone who worked with him—regardless of whether they liked him or not—knew deep down that he was indeed special. During his first week, he danced a *pas de deux* (a dance for two performers) from the classic ballet *Giselle*. Visiting dancers and critics noticed him at once, and word spread quickly that the Kirov was nurturing a new discovery.

For the young and very serious Baryshnikov, it seemed that everything was going his way. Besides his favored status in the ballet company, he loved living in the city of Leningrad. He continued to study under Pushkin even after his three-year course of formal school study was over, and he devoured his teacher's knowledge eagerly. Pushkin was both a mentor and something of a father figure for the young dancer. The two remained close friends until Pushkin died of a heart attack on the streets of Leningrad in 1970. It was undoubtedly Pushkin's wealth of knowledge, his classical orientation, and his ability to connect with Misha that made him the dancer's first great influence.

Alexander Pushkin's legacy to Baryshnikov went beyond dance. He also passed on an intellectual curiosity and an interest in Western culture. The young dancer witnessed his teacher's dissatisfaction with the country's closemindedness and isolationism. Baryshnikov also began cultivating those feelings. But unlike Pushkin, Misha's feelings would eventually cause him to dramatically change the course of his life.

Baryshnikov became known early on for his flying leaps and acrobatic style of dance.

CHAPTER 2

LENINGRAD'S EMERGING STAR

*The audience must be made to feel that the
stage is not big enough to hold the dancer.
That's the source of tension and excitement.*
—Mikhail Baryshnikov

At the time of Baryshnikov's debut as a soloist,
the Kirov dance company was still considered by most
to be the best classical ballet company in the world.
Most classical ballets are based on famous stories that
use well-established characters, dance steps, and dance
styles. Ballets—such as *Giselle, Swan Lake,
The Nutcracker,* and *Don Quixote*—have fairly rigid
guidelines by which a company or a dancer can inter-
pret the action. (Modern ballet, on the other hand,
relies less on telling a story and focuses mostly on
new and original works. The emphasis is often on the
beauty of the motion of dance rather than on interpret-
ing a "story" with dancing actors. Much of modern

ballet shuns complicated, detailed costumes and sets in favor of simple elements that highlight the dancers.)

By the beginning of the seventies, however, many thought of the Kirov as too old-fashioned. Bound by tradition, some said it lagged behind its peers in creativity, ingenuity, and vitality. More restricted by the traditional choreography and the more classical repertoire than its competitor—the Bolshoi Ballet—the Kirov refused to match the more extravagant and athletic style of its rival.

Much of the Kirov's stagnation was attributed to the artistic direction of Konstantin Sergeyev. Eager to please his superiors and friends higher up in the Communist Party, Sergeyev maintained a dull, lifeless repertoire, the primary purpose of which was to glorify the state. As with most other art forms in the Soviet Union at the time, there were well-established themes and messages that were allowed to be expressed in performances and interpretations of ballet, opera, and theater. Each of the arts was overseen by a committee of Party members who monitored the messages of the works being performed. As long as those messages glorified the communist ideals, or defamed the principles of capitalism, they were allowed. Needless to say, the narrow margin of acceptability allowed by the various governing groups made for a cultural environment that lacked spontaneity and freedom.

The rigidity of expression carried over to the typecasting of dancers. Members of the troupe were classified fairly strictly and quite quickly by the artistic management of the Kirov Ballet. A dancer's body type as well as physical capabilities determined whether one would spend an entire career as a *danseur noble* (leading man) or as a demi-caractére (character actor). Musculature was also an important factor in deciding which roles one danced. Big-boned, broad-shouldered men played the heroic roles, and the graceful, curving, longish men played the romantic roles. Good dancers with unremarkable looks and, perhaps, expressive faces were given the character parts to dance. These strict categories were employed with the belief that they helped to preserve the integrity of the ballet. The classifications also quickly defined which ballets a dancer would dance and which would never be offered—even with a lifetime of training.

Technique and ability did not play a part in deciding which roles young Baryshnikov danced—he was clearly capable of dancing anything. His amazing versatility, in addition to his rather unique look and body type, made him hard to classify. His long, sleek muscles and soft *plié* (knee bend) seemed to make him perfectly suited to the romantic characters. But his lack of great height and his boyish face—capable of being both pretty and clownish—suited him to some roles as a *demi-caractère*.

Baryshnikov's style and technique were molded and developed strictly by the standard Soviet methods. These methods, however, periodically swung back and forth between two styles, which have been favored in the Soviet Union and around the world. One style stresses the beauty of perfectly executed movement. The other style focuses on the more emotional, interpretive, and poetic aspects of dance, drawing on the combination of dancing with acting and less on the perfect execution of an arm movement or *pirouette* (spin or spins of the entire body). Baryshnikov fell most comfortably into the first category of dancer. His execution was so precise that the thrill of watching him dance was derived from the beauty in his flawless execution of movements that no other dancer could perform as precisely. His athletic feats were unequaled, as Hubert Saal of *Newsweek* wrote: "With his great levitation, his soaring leaps, he seems more at home in the air than on the ground." For Baryshnikov, perfect technique was his trademark. Rudolf Nureyev, on the other hand, made up for what he lacked in perfect technique with a great expressive quality and emotion that Baryshnikov has yet to match.

The fact that Misha was so young yet so advanced in technique made it hard for him to find challenging roles and made it difficult to pair him successfully with partners. Even his 1967 debut at the Kirov, in which Misha danced the difficult Peasant *pas de deux* from *Giselle's* first act, appeared effortless for the young virtuoso. During much of his early career, the years 1967 to 1969, he was saddled with dancing the part of romantic young men who symbolized the hope and youthfulness of Russia but did little to stimulate the creative impulses of the dancer himself.

In 1968, a renegade choreographer named Igor Tchernichov presented Baryshnikov with a project that did, indeed, spark the young dancer's creative impulses. The choreographer took up an innovative production of *Romeo and Juliet* and wanted Misha to be his Mercutio. Tchernichov's vision of the piece entailed partly classical, partly modern choreography that was both striking and erotic. As the project took shape, it was shot down by the Kirov's art committee. But Tchernichov did not give up. Irina Kolpakova was soon enlisted to dance the part of Juliet, which greatly boosted the overall stature of the project. As a very well-respected ballerina, Kolpakova was also influential with Communist Party members in the upper echelons. Accomplished dancers achieved power and influence by distinguishing the Soviet Union's artistic productions. Thus, high-profile dancers like

Sergeyev (left) and Dudinskaya in the Kirov Ballet production of *Swan Lake*.

Kolpakova were very valuable to Party members who were responsible for maintaining the precious image of Soviet dominance in ballet. It was always in the Party's best interest to keep the most famous dancers as happy as possible. Because of this Kolpakova was able to persuade both the Party members and the Kirov's art committee to feature *Romeo and Juliet* in a special gala evening performance sponsored by the Kirov.

The new ballet was ready by December of 1969. The choreography was bold, innovative, sensual, and quite different from the standard fare presented by the Kirov. On December 30, *Romeo and Juliet* premiered and stunned its audience with delight. Despite its enthusiastic reception, however, the ballet was only performed once. Kolpakova convinced all concerned that it would be better not to risk the continuation of a production that could possibly irritate Party members with unique and unconventional visions of ballet.

The production did, however, spark a new collaboration between Baryshnikov and Tchernichov, leading them to work together on Ravel's *Bolero* in 1969. During this rehearsal process, Misha and Tchernichov would spur each other's creativity with dance combinations, new possibilities, and unique interpretations of characters. This creative partnership was the first time he had felt truly excited about the potential of ballet since his innocent days with Pushkin.

Unfortunately, *Bolero* ran into the same resistance that plagued *Romeo and Juliet*. The ballet was banned by the Kirov. After this disappointment, Misha grew more impatient with the staunch conservatism and narrow-mindedness shown by the company. Sergeyev, the director of the Kirov, fostered this conventionalism to show his unwavering support for the traditional aesthetics of the Soviet ballet. But he also had personal reasons for squelching Tchernichov's efforts, mostly springing from jealousy and past rivalries.

For Baryshnikov, the politics and stuffiness of the Kirov company was beginning to feel like a serious hindrance. The young dancer wanted to dance many different roles, to experience as many facets of ballet as he could, but it seemed he would constantly be held back. Rather than being excited and fired up about new projects, Baryshnikov found himself feeling bored with his work in the troupe. Though Misha saw no alternatives at that point in his life, he did resolve to keep searching for opportunities that would enable him to explore his art with the enthusiasm he craved.

Baryshnikov won a gold medal at the Moscow International Ballet Competition in June, 1969.

CHAPTER 3

THE KIROV'S YOUNGEST HOPE

Baryshnikov is probably the most dazzling virtuoso we've seen. He is more spectacular in sheer technique than any other male dancer. What he actually does, no one can really define. His steps are in no ballet dictionary. And he seems to be able to stop in mid-air and sit in space.
—Dance Critic Walter Terry

By the time he finished his third season at the Kirov in 1969, Baryshnikov was the undisputed star of the company. But fame in the Soviet Union is quite different from fame in America. Stardom does not mean great wealth, television appearances, product endorsements, commercials, or merchandising of one's image. Soviet fame means, above all, respect and admiration from one's country and its open acknowledgement of one's worth. Often, with great status comes more comfortable living accommodations—such as a large apartment with modern appliances and a maid—and access to specialty foods and personal care products not available in the public markets. But even as a star by the beginning of the seventies, Baryshnikov was still sharing bare rooms with other dancers and relying on the Kirov and its sponsor, the government, for financial support.

A professional relationship with many of the Soviet Union's greatest artists was an advantage Misha gained as his reputation grew. He especially benefited from meeting other great dancers. One of those dancers was Natalia Makarova. As they worked together on the Kirov productions, the two dancers' professional relationship turned into a romantic one. Not much is known about the particulars of this relationship, but it is clear that throughout his career, Baryshnikov has been particularly prone to romances with other dancers. Of course, this is not surprising given the great amount of time dancers in a troupe spend with each other, leaving little time for a social life outside of dance. Baryshnikov, however, has seemed most interested in those women with whom he has danced the best. Or, perhaps, he dances his best with those women because he is the most interested in them.

Another aspect of Baryshnikov's fame that gained him some special advantage was his exposure to great choreographers, composers, and writers. As Misha emerged as a great talent, many Soviet artists yearned to create pieces especially for him. One such person was choreographer Leonid Yakobson, who was known as a colorful rebel. Yakobson's style was unconventional. It often incorporated pantomime, caricature (exaggerations and humorous distortions), and neo-modernist dance movements (non-classical, choppy, and disjointed steps) as the basis for its communication. The choreographer hoped to sharpen the expressiveness of his ballet and strived to make it more emotional and visually exciting.

Leonid Yakobson was well known for his unconventional choreography.

Yakobson's bold, fresh vision excited Misha. As he became more and more tired of the predictable Kirov roles, Baryshnikov yearned to work with choreographers who had new visions that would allow him to explore his talents. A ballet entitled *Vestris*, created by Yakobson expressly for Baryshnikov, offered the dancer just such an opportunity.

Baryshnikov danced the lead role in *Vestris* for the Moscow International Ballet Competition in 1969. The reaction was overwhelming. Dance critics, as well as judges and audience members, hailed his performance as brilliant. The choreography, too, was praised for its richness and its expressiveness as well as its innovation. Though the dancing and the choreography were, indeed, exceptional, some of the warm response to the work may have been owed to the fact that it was performed in Moscow and not in Leningrad at the Kirov. Moscow had a reputation as being a bit more open and worldly in its view, whereas Leningrad (and the Kirov that represented it) always appeared to favor the more conventional and traditional.

The judges at the international competition were some of the most renowned in all of ballet. Maya Plisetskaya, a world famous ballerina, became an instant fan of Baryshnikov's after seeing his *Vestris* at the competition. Out of a possible twelve rating points for his performance, Plisetskaya gave Misha thirteen. The ballerina marveled at his technique, his lightness in the air, and his amazing ease at combining classical movements with grotesque pantomime. She also noticed the dancer's strong acting gift. His movements and facial expressions were as convincing and compelling as his dancing. Plisetskaya, along with the other judges, awarded Baryshnikov a gold medal for *Vestris*.

Once in a while, dancers from the Kirov were allowed to leave the country to tour with their troupe in other cities. Often, these trips abroad would expose the dancers to other influences—other governments— and would make them less satisfied with their lives in the USSR. The Kirov's August 1970 tour of London gave Baryshnikov his first exposure to a Western city. The opportunity afforded him a taste of Western culture—he went to see *Fiddler on the Roof, Jesus Christ Superstar,* and the movie version of *West Side Story,* and bought his first Simon and Garfunkel album. He

Baryshnikov

A PICTURE PORTFOLIO

Baryshnikov practicing with Susan Jaffe for their performance in *Giselle* (1982), Mikhail's signature ballet.

(*Below*)
Baryshnikov catches ballerina Cynthia Harvey in their American Ballet Theater performance of *Don Quixote* (1983).

Mikhail tap dancing with his co-star Gregory Hines in the movie *White Nights* (1985).

Joyce Herring and Baryshnikov dance together in the modern ballet *El Penitente* (1988).

saw a modern-dance company for the first time, as well as a jazz dance class. Before this trip, the young Russian had hardly even stopped to think that those forms of dance existed.

His trip to England provided him with another special opportunity: he met Rudolf Nureyev, then considered the most exciting male dancer in the world. His meeting with Nureyev—who was considered a criminal in the USSR for his defection in 1961—was accomplished without the knowledge of the tour's chaperones, who certainly would not have approved. After being smuggled out in a car one morning, Baryshnikov spent the entire day with Nureyev, talking about dance, choreography, technique, working in London, and, most importantly, about Pushkin and his wife. Nureyev was anxious to hear about the couple who had been so good to him.

The realities of defection first became clear to Baryshnikov during his London trip. During his visit with Nureyev, he saw how the dancer lived and what his freedom was actually like. Much of what the young Russian saw—antique French furniture, a lavish home, and material luxury—was beyond anything that Misha had ever envisioned for a simple dancer. But more importantly, he also saw a man who could dance any ballet he wished, whenever he wanted, and in any country he wished.

It was also while the Kirov was in London that Natalia Makarova, Baryshnikov's former partner, defected from the company, asking England for political asylum. Baryshnikov was shocked by her defection. He still could not imagine leaving his country, his teachers, his family, and his audience.

During the Kirov tour of London, still more acclaim was heaped on Baryshnikov. English critics pronounced him a genius and hailed him as one of the

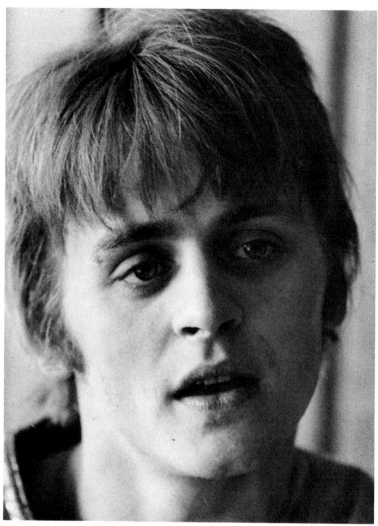
Baryshnikov in 1970 at Festival Hall, in London.

greatest talents to ever dance on the stage. This praise showed Baryshnikov that his talent was, indeed, recognized outside of Russia. He recalls, "I really understood that people liked me not just in Leningrad . . . that they also appreciated my level in the West."

Back in the Soviet Union, however, the Kirov's repertoire continued to stifle Baryshnikov's creativity and enthusiasm. The version of *Hamlet* staged that year by Sergeyev was yet another in the Kirov's string of predictable productions. The ballet won a prize from the government for the best ballet of the year, but rather than inspiring Misha, it stood as just another example of state mediocrity. In fact, the dancer became embarrassed by the production and called it—as others in the cast did—a "choreographic void." Nonetheless, Soviet officials pronounced *Hamlet* a great achievement, and Sergeyev's supporters in the Party quickly squelched any criticism of it within the ballet community. Fed up with the charade surrounding this work, Baryshnikov dropped out of the production after two performances—something he had never done before.

In 1970, personal disappointment followed Misha's professional unhappiness. That year Alexander Pushkin died. Pushkin had been more of a father to Misha in many ways, than his real father, who Misha only spoke to once or twice a year. "I was totally on my own," Baryshnikov remembers after he lost Pushkin.

The Kirov mounted a few more disappointing productions before Misha was offered a role that excited him. Sergei Yursky, a leading Soviet actor, wanted Baryshnikov to play the toreador in the television version of the Ernest Hemingway novel *The Sun Also Rises*. Intrigued by an opportunity to display his acting talent, Baryshnikov accepted the part. Many actors were outraged that a dancer would be cast in a nondance role, and almost everyone was convinced that the ballet star would fail miserably. But Misha proved his doubters wrong. He was very well received in the part and showed a great natural ability in front of the camera.

More television work fell into line for Baryshnikov soon after the Hemingway story was complete. Choreographer Kirill Laskari cast Misha in a made-

Rudolf Nureyev and Margot Fonteyn rehearse *Pelleas et Melisande* in 1969.

for-television ballet entitled *The Tale of Serf Nikishka*. Though the ballet was good, the camera work and direction did not take into account how the large, theatrical gestures of ballet would translate to the extremely close and intimate eye of the television camera. Thus, much of Baryshnikov's performance seemed over-theatrical and did not show his dancing in the best possible light.

After completing his television work in 1971, Misha returned to the stage in a ballet entitled *The Creation of the World*—choreographed by two of the Bolshoi's most gifted artists, Natalia Kasatkina and Vladimir Vasiliov. Based on the biblical story of creation, the choreography was lively, irreverent, and quite humorous in many instances. By Soviet standards, the production was downright radical. The action showed God, bored, playing a game with the Devil to pass the time. The role offered Baryshnikov, who played Adam, some unique opportunities to perform a humorous, wide-eyed, innocent character.

The Creation of the World proved to be a significant production in many ways. First, the story and the choreography of the ballet were something of a departure for the Soviet stage, and thus marked a breakthrough for less traditional staging. Second, Baryshnikov's performance in the piece showed a perfect combination of demanding physical ability, acting talent, and humor. Critics and experts in the field were quick to praise the dancer's achievements and to recognize Baryshnikov as a true virtuoso. The final significance of *Creation* was the fact that, after the first few performances, much of the cast was never again seen on a Soviet stage. For various reasons, many of *Creation's* dancers defected from Russia or dropped out of the dance world shortly after the ballet's debut, due to personal or emotional conflicts.

Baryshnikov dances the Peasant *pas de deux* from *Giselle*, with Bolshakova, in 1970.

CHAPTER 4

TURNING POINTS

Baryshnikov is a one-man theatrical event that nearly defies summary. He is an unbelievable technician with invisible technique. Most dancers, even the great ones, make obvious preliminaries to leaps. He simply floats into confounding feats of acrobatics and then comes to a still, collected repose.
—*Time* cover story

Though he was well aware that he was regarded as a genius dancer, Baryshnikov still felt the need to prove to the Kirov seniors that he could act well enough to dance such classics as *Giselle* and *Swan Lake* on a regular basis. The role of Albrecht in *Giselle* is one of ballet's greatest male roles, and Baryshnikov wanted to make his mark on it. Albrecht had been traditionally portrayed as a repentant villain who asks for forgiveness for tricking a young woman and causing her death. During the political and cultural thaw of the 1960s under Khrushchev's administration, new interpretations of Albrecht appeared, most notably the one created by Nureyev. This new portrayal transformed *Giselle* into a more complex psychological drama and focused on Albrecht as a tormented intellectual confused by his own motivations and desires. Nureyev's Albrecht character uses Giselle's death as a way to reassess himself and his own life.

Given the role's past history, Baryshnikov's interpretation of Albrecht was all the more striking. At his debut performance in 1972, Alla Sizova danced Giselle to Misha's Albrecht—who dazzled all. In the dancer's own book, *Baryshnikov at Work,* he explained that he chose Albrecht's sincere love for Giselle, rather than his repentance, as the key to the part. His Albrecht was youthful and enthusiastic and overflowed with love for Giselle.

Act 1 of *Giselle* involved very little dancing for Albrecht but allowed Baryshnikov a chance to do a good deal of acting. Since true, honest love drives the character (not lust or passion), Albrecht does not feel that he has betrayed Giselle when she learns he is a count and is engaged to another woman. He truly believes that their love will make everything all right. When Giselle dies, Albrecht is stunned but not repentant. Baryshnikov's Albrecht, upon hearing the news of the death, did not run offstage (as all past Albrechts had done), but rather stood motionless, stunned and frozen. This one small action had enormous interpretative significance. Baryshnikov's choice here, as in many other moments in the ballet, was unique and made his portrayal of the character a true work of creativity.

The second act of *Giselle* was an even greater departure from the standard interpretations. The story shows that since her death, Giselle has become Albrecht's unobtainable ideal. When he shows up at the grave, Giselle appears with a group of dancing ghosts who, like her, spend their eternal lives dancing.

Albrecht is forced to dance by the ghosts and their queen, Myrtha. He is compelled to perform a rigorous series of steps that require great quickness, stamina, technique, and strength. In the past, the male dancers who had played Albrecht simply wanted to survive the ordeal. This was not how Baryshnikov saw the part. His Albrecht danced the demanding steps with determination, trueness, and a great energy to demonstrate to Giselle and the ghosts the sincerity of his love.

Though Baryshnikov's interpretive abilities were well exercised in *Giselle*, it was not enough to satisfy him as an artist. By 1972, Misha's feelings of stagnation made him seriously pursue a move from the Kirov to the Bolshoi Ballet in Moscow. The Bolshoi was the Soviet Union's other great ballet company, the only other held in as high regard as the Kirov. Baryshnikov spoke with the Bolshoi's choreographer about the possibility of a move but nothing ever came of their discussions. There were, perhaps, many reasons the Bolshoi turned down the opportunity to have one of the world's greatest dancers join its ranks. Among them were fears of disrupting the other dancers in the company—making them jealous or threatening their status. In addition, many at the Bolshoi thought Baryshnikov was too refined, too classical for the big, muscular, athletic ballets they tended to perform. Baryshnikov's rejection by the Bolshoi was probably in his best interest anyway, for their burly style of dance would have offered him little opportunity to use the incredible talents he had.

The episode with the Bolshoi demonstrated one important thing to Baryshnikov: in the Soviet Union even a great dancer is tied to one stage. There are too many dangers in letting him roam, particularly if he is the dancer upon whom much of the success of the company and the choreographer/director depends.

The Bolshoi was the rival company to the Kirov and tended to do more muscular and athletic productions. Here, a scene from *The Little Humpbacked Horse* is performed.

Baryshnikov was largely responsible for the present status of the Kirov, and this was an important tool for Sergeyev to use in seeking approval from the Party for achievements in the arts. For these reasons, it is no surprise that the Bolshoi was hesitant to bring about a change. And it followed that Misha was seldom allowed to tour out of the country or to dance with other companies. He was simply trapped.

Constant dissatisfaction now plagued Baryshnikov. The dancer felt he had attained a new level of sophistication in his dance but had also reached an artistic dead end. He felt he had met all the challenges given him. At the same time, Misha began to feel even more uneasy with being watched by the secret police. The KGB constantly watched artists, monitoring their attitudes and loyalties toward the Soviet Union. He suspected that his apartment was being monitored and that his phone was tapped. And he knew that the more unhappy he became, the more he would be watched. At the Kirov (as well as the Bolshoi, undoubtedly) a number of dancers were hired as informants who reported any suspicious conversations or actions by their colleagues. This atmosphere caused him to become very secretive. He could not confide in any of his friends or colleagues about his problems for fear that they would be pressured into informing the KGB about his dissatisfaction.

This uneasiness came soon after Natalia Makarova had defected. Her defection dealt an embarrassing blow to the KGB. (Such an embarrassment had not arisen since 1961, when Russia's highest profile dancer—Rudolf Nureyev—slipped through the fingers of the secret police while on tour.) The Makarova defection showed much more than the KGB bungling a job, however. It also convinced many members of the Party that the people in charge were losing the ideological hold on the arts and its artists. The defection pointed out the inferior information coming from various informants within the Kirov and was all the more ironic due to the fact that Makarova escaped because the KGB was so closely watching Baryshnikov at the time.

As was the Soviet ritual, an eventual scapegoat had to be found to blame for the ballerina's escape. The scapegoat turned out to be Sergeyev, a relatively powerless man who had lost many of his Party friends when Khrushchev took power. Once Sergeyev was targeted, his days as head of the Kirov were literally numbered. Soon, his behavior was called into question and his work was scrutinized. After Sergeyev was dismissed from the Kirov, the company began to deteriorate even more rapidly than it had before.

A trio of three fairly respected dancers, Irina Kolpakova, Vladilen Semenov, and Oleg Vinogradov, tried to save the drowning ballet company by taking charge in 1971. Unfortunately, the new leaders could not agree on policies or ideas, and the organization of the company continued to decline. Other artistic directors were brought in to no avail. Igor Belsky, who arrived in 1973—though hard-working and dedicated—was almost laughably incompetent as a leader. Misha's low opinion of Belsky only made his situation seem more intolerable.

It was under Belsky's leadership that Baryshnikov first started work on what was known as a "special evening" of his own. Misha was the youngest dancer to ever receive the rare "special evening" opportunity. It was a unique chance for him to put together a program that would showcase his own particular talents. In most cases, a dancer was allowed to choose his or her own pieces and to present new work never before performed. Though these evenings often went against Party wishes, they were tolerated as a sign of open-

Natalia Makarova defected to the West in 1970 despite being closely watched by the KGB.

ness and good public relations abroad. When Baryshnikov's special evening was approved, he decided to focus entirely on original work, created especially for him. He employed choreographers who were not in official favor, those on the fringe who were outside the regular circles but who were allowed to work.

Baryshnikov spent the entire winter of 1973–1974 trying to put together his special evening, but the rare opportunity soon turned into a frustrating ordeal. Many of the colleagues Misha approached for help and collaboration turned him down. Some dancers were still hurt by slights and insults they suffered under Sergeyev at the Kirov. Others were unwilling to be part of such a risky collection of material. Still others were simply jealous of the notoriety Baryshnikov had achieved and were not enthusiastic about helping him to enhance it further.

When Misha finally collected a group of artists for the evening, rehearsals were plagued by personal and artistic disputes. Dancers dropped out, ballets were changed, and concepts were constantly overhauled. By the time of dress rehearsal, Baryshnikov was completely defeated and depressed by the state of his material. Nothing seemed to work. The sets were wrong. The costumes felt silly. And even though the critics were very favorable, Misha felt sorely disappointed.

His feelings of failure caused Baryshnikov to spend most of the spring of 1974 alone and unmotivated to do anything. His lack of direction and his frustration with the system caused him to wonder about other alternatives. It was at this point that thoughts of defection first entered the dancer's head. But even with all the pain he was experiencing, the thought of actually giving up his entire life and friends was too frightening for him to contemplate. His friends, though he considered only two or three people his friends at the time, were an important emotional support system for him—even more than his father or stepsiblings. "The difference between Americans and Russians," Baryshnikov once said, "is that Americans go to their shrink, and Russians go to their friends." No matter how aggravated he became with the ballet system, he couldn't avoid the fact that the Soviet

Union still had all the people in the world with whom he felt some bond. He also felt, as many of his peers did, that the USSR was still his home, and it must be accepted with all its shortcomings. And, how could he be sure that the outside world would recognize him as a great talent? What if he could not survive out in a world he had hardly been allowed to experience? These questions rolled around Misha's mind for months.

In the meantime—in what would turn out to be his final performance in the Soviet Union—Baryshnikov danced Albrecht once again on the Kirov stage. This time, however, he portrayed the character more dramatically, with a haunting sense of sadness and new desperation that seemed incredibly real.

Baryshnikov in the "Don Quixote" *pas de deux* in 1970.

CHAPTER 5

THE GREAT LEAP

With his fantastic talent, sitting around at the Kirov is simply suicide—he'll choke on the routine.
—Roland Petit, Choreographer

With the disappointment of his "special evening" still fresh in his mind—and his general feeling of stagnation at the Kirov—Baryshnikov began to feel more restless than ever before. He began to think about dancing abroad, about the excitement of touring and absorbing new influences and cultures. The twenty-six-year-old star's restlessness did not escape the notice of the KGB and, in fact, it made them quite nervous. Baryshnikov was a monumental talent, now known the world over, who was a valuable symbol of Russian superiority in ballet. Even though the young dancer had been expressing his desire to travel for a while, his wishes met with resistance that seemed hard to overcome. Finally, partly in an effort to appease Baryshnikov, a company trip to Italy was planned.

In 1974, choreographer Roland Petit came to Leningrad with his Ballet de Marseille to perform their version of *Notre Dame de Paris.* On opening night, Baryshnikov had an opportunity to meet Petit. Both gentlemen had heard of one another before the meeting, and both had great respect for each other's work. Baryshnikov and Petit became good friends that night, and their instant liking for each other paved the way for possible collaborations in the future.

While still in Leningrad, the Petits were invited to dinner at Baryshnikov's comfortable but simply furnished apartment near the Moika Canal. Supper was a traditional Russian collection of fresh black caviar, cold veal in lingonberry sauce, marinated mushrooms, Georgian wine, and cognac from Armenia. It was during this dinner that Petit softly encouraged Misha to consider the possibility of staying in Europe during the upcoming Kirov tour of Italy. Baryshnikov did not respond to this directly and kept his thoughts to himself. Though his close friends knew of his growing impatience in the Soviet Union, even his closest confidants were not told of his plans. Some of his silence was due to the fact that he was afraid his apartment was bugged by the KGB. But he also didn't want anyone he left behind to have any knowledge that could prove dangerous to them once he was gone, if he did decide to defect.

Petit's visit and the prospect of future projects with him brought Misha closer to a decision about defection. By the spring of 1974, he was quietly asking close friends if they thought he had a chance at being successful in New York. But the trip to Italy would not be the one that separated Baryshnikov from his homeland. That trip would come in June.

In June 1974, a small troupe of the Soviet Union's most acclaimed dancers, many from the Bolshoi, were given an opportunity to tour Canada. The tour, which included Baryshnikov, came about despite great resistance from the KGB. It was the iron-clad assurance of the Party's favorite ballerina, Irina Kolpakova, that everyone would safely return which finally enabled the tour to be approved. Yet, everyone involved was very nervous. And as soon as Misha left for Canada, a lively debate—almost a public bet—took place in Moscow and Leningrad between those who were convinced Baryshnikov would return and those who were certain the Soviet Union would never again see its native son.

At the beginning of the tour, while in Montreal, audiences gave Baryshnikov and his troupe standing ovations and dance critics gave them rave reviews. Dance critic Arlene Croce, of *The New Yorker*, wrote of the Soviet phenomenon, "Baryshnikov is able to perform unparalleled spectacular feats as an extension of classical rather than character or acrobatic dancing. . . . He gets into a step sequence more quickly, complicates it more variously, and prolongs it more extravagantly than any other dancer I have ever seen."

The dancer's immediate acceptance by the media and the dance community—accompanied by overwhelming praise for his talent—was not enough to take his mind off his unhappiness with his situation. Misha's decision to defect while in Canada was an unplanned, somewhat improvised and spontaneous idea that he was not completely sure of even as he was doing it. Baryshnikov himself once said that almost all of the major decisions of his life "have been made in a split second," and this was no exception. He compares his sudden decision to what happens when a couple splits up.

Sometimes it takes years for this to make sense, and sometimes, when you realize it's the end, you have to make a decision instantly, because you can't physically continue to keep doing what you're doing. You must turn from the very firm and nice road to the swamp. I realized that I didn't want to live in Russia; I didn't want to dance in the [Kirov]. I didn't like the way people treated each other. You had to pretend something you didn't feel.

It was true that Misha felt severely constrained by the Soviet system and worried that his talent would never be fully realized at the Kirov. And he did long for freedom and a chance to explore new territory with his art. But defection also meant that he would never again see his Russian friends or family. It meant he would have to leave behind everything he owned, everything he knew, *forever*. In addition, defection meant that he would become a criminal under Soviet law, punishable with a maximum of fifteen years in prison if he ever returned.

On June 29, the company was performing in Toronto. By the end of the matinee performance, officials in the Canadian government had been notified of Baryshnikov's request for political asylum and a lawyer, Jim Peterson, had made all the legal arrangements. Misha decided that his move would be made after his evening performance—the last performance the company would have in Toronto before they left for Vancouver the next day.

Baryshnikov left his room on the night of June 29 and headed for the theater. He was terribly nervous and, as he walked, he could feel his hands shaking uncontrollably. Immediately, he stopped to compose himself. He could not allow his anxiety to arouse any suspicion on the part of the tour leaders. It would take only one phone call to Moscow from a tour leader who felt uneasy to have Baryshnikov on a plane that night, flying home in the interest of safety. Calling on every

Baryshnikov arriving in the United States after his defection in Toronto.

bit of acting ability he possessed, he headed to the theater and prepared for the performance.

His last performance with his Russian colleagues—the *pas de deux* from *Don Quixote*—seemed unusually brilliant and inspired. The audience could sense a tortured uneasiness in Baryshnikov's steps, a tragic inner conflict in his character that had never been there before.

As Misha performed *Don Quixote,* friends were sitting in a nearby restaurant waiting to meet him and to take him to a safe place. The lawyer, Peterson, had a car parked nearby that would take Misha to a temporary hiding place. Unfortunately, his friends were not aware that the performance had begun late (due to a technical problem with the curtain). They waited, in anguish, not knowing what had happened.

There was a farewell party planned for the troupe in Toronto, and Misha's attendance was, of course, required. He was to be met by the troupe leaders in a car at the backstage door after the show. When his curtain call was complete, Baryshnikov flew into his dressing room, changed his clothes, and quickly headed for an exit. Pushing his way through an excited crowd of fans, he finally made it out onto the street. Once outside, he began to walk faster.

A colleague's voice called out "Misha, where are you going?"

"To the corner to say goodbye to some friends," was the dancer's trembling answer. "I'll be right back."

At this point Baryshnikov broke into a run. A gang of fans behind him followed, thinking he was fleeing them. His mind raced as he rushed into the darkness—confused and without any idea of where he was. Misha recalls, "When I started to run, I didn't feel my legs under me, I just felt fear and an empty stomach." He ran out into a street and was almost hit by a car. Luckily, a concerned friend had left the restaurant and had headed for the theater to check things out. As the friend walked, he was nearly run down by the fleeing dancer, wide-eyed, breathless, and terrified. The friend immediately hailed a taxi, both got in, and Misha was taken to a hidden apartment where he would be safe. "I almost threw up when I jumped into that car," he remembers.

By that evening, everyone involved in the mission—particularly Misha—had consumed a great deal of vodka, both to celebrate and to numb the pain. Baryshnikov was unusually moody, feeling at once both elation and great sadness. It would take several years before Misha could speak openly about his defection, even to his closest friends. Now, he looks back on his ordeal with mixed emotions:

> I never dreamed I would do it. I was in the hotel in Toronto looking at the open sky, and it came upon me like a volcano, like a revelation. I have no doubts about what I did, but I have regrets. I left behind my friends, my public, my theater, and Leningrad, my city, the most beautiful in the world. Now I have a divided soul.

Misha spent a good deal of his first night of freedom on the telephone. Most importantly, he spoke with his old partner Natalia Makarova, who had defected in 1970 and was dancing with the American Ballet Theatre (ABT). During their conversation, Makarova promised her old friend that she would waste no time convincing Lucia Chase at the ABT in New York to include Canada's newest ballet sensation immediately in their schedule.

As Misha fell asleep that night, fear and great expectation filled him at the same time, making him uncertain about his future. But there was now one thing of which he was certain—he could never go back to his country.

Baryshnikov with Natalia Makarova in American Ballet Theatre's production of *La Sylphide*.

CHAPTER 6

STIRRING UP AMERICA

*To relax is difficult for me. I know it is important
to have a sensible schedule and not to exaggerate,
but I am like a horse used to pulling a great load.
I can't begin to think of what would happen if I
stopped dancing. I have to squelch those thoughts,
drive them down. The stage is a form of opium
for me—a psychological feeling I must have.
I cannot be without.*
—Mikhail Baryshnikov

Not long after his defection, Canadian journalists
discovered where Baryshnikov was staying. The day
after the dancer left his troupe, the news stories began
coming out. For privacy and safety, Misha was moved
to a secluded island where he could recover from his
ordeal as he pursued one of his favorite pastimes:
fishing. But even a beautiful private retreat was not
enough to prevent the insomnia and nightmares that
plagued him for weeks after his defection. He got a
severe rash, which was almost certainly brought on by
pure anxiety.

At the height of his misery came an invitation from
Canadian television to dance *La Sylphide.* Excited by

the challenge of dancing a role he had never danced before, and feeling a desire to do something for the country that took him in, Baryshnikov accepted. In addition to being a great success, the *La Sylphide* project provided a perfect vehicle to lift the dancer out of his funk by distracting him with work.

A few weeks later Baryshnikov was in New York, dancing *Giselle* for the American Ballet Theatre (ABT). It was the first ballet he performed with an entire company in the West, and his first reunion with Natalia Makarova since her London defection in 1970. *The New York Times* critic Anna Kisselgoff evaluated ABT's newest member after his Western debut:

> There are two types of great male dancers. Some do not conceal the heroic preparation and effort involved in the most demanding virtuoso feats and derive their very impact from this exciting climax—of difficulties visibly surmounted. Then there are those who purposely strive to go beyond technique and, concentrating on stylistic purity, conceal their own virtuosity.
>
> Mr. Baryshnikov, as he has shown in the past and now in his two brief solos in Act II, is a unique blend of both types. The extraordinary difficulty of the steps he executed (such as the double assemblé that only less than a handful of dancers in the world can do) was evident. At the same time, while the virtuosity was visible, it appeared to be without effort.
>
> Above all, there was a consistency of classical style at every instant that will truly be Mr. Baryshnikov's own special contribution to male dancing in the West.

Despite his enthusiastic welcome and praise in the United States, Baryshnikov's new life required a great adjustment. First, he had to be assured that, indeed, Westerners would recognize his talent and would accord him the same status as a dancer that he had enjoyed in the Soviet Union. The recognition he received, of course, turned out to be even greater than that in the USSR. Second, the dancer now had many more career choices confronting him. And now the

Makarova celebrates the publication of her autobiography with
her favorite co-star in 1979.

choices were his to make. With that freedom came a new responsibility for his life and success, and, if he failed, there would only be himself—not the Kirov—to blame. Third, there were some problems with Natalia Makarova. It seemed the ballerina expected Baryshnikov to be the same dancer he was years before, somewhat accommodating and attentive to her, and willing to do whatever she wished. It is also possible that Makarova had hopes of rekindling the old dance-romance partnership they enjoyed in the Soviet Union and was bitter when Baryshnikov was not interested. Unfortunately for her, the boy had become a man—an independent and determined man—and was no longer willing to adjust his career to the needs of others. Besides, Misha wanted to dance with a new interest, a delicate woman named Gelsey Kirkland, a fine ballerina with the New York City Ballet (NYCB), who was beautifully suited to his style. Once again, Baryshnikov would become romantically involved with a successful dance partner.

Baryshnikov called Kirkland and asked her to join the company at ABT. This request was something of a shock for the young ballerina, particularly because she barely knew Baryshnikov. Kirkland recalls, "When we toured in Russia I shook his hand, watched one class, one rehearsal, and one performance. He was the best dancer I ever saw, maybe that ever was."

It did not take long for Kirkland to accept Baryshnikov's offer, though it did mean she had to leave the exciting NYCB company, which was under the brilliant directorship of George Balanchine. But Kirkland felt a move was still the right thing for her to do. "Maybe I was too comfortable in that company," she reflected later. "I felt I had to make a change. I really did want to dance the classic ballets. I was 21, a pivotal time. Ballets like *Giselle* needed acting techniques and concepts that I hadn't learned."

Gelsey Kirkland had a romantic as well as a professional attachment to Baryshnikov.

Somehow, Misha must have had an instinct about Gelsey Kirkland, for he felt certain the two of them would make a mesmerizing pair on stage. It didn't take long for the rest of the world to see that Baryshnikov's instinct was exactly right. Performing together—Misha with his regal Russian technique and

Gelsey with her carefree, expressive American training—they were a sublime combination of both the
Eastern and the Western dance traditions.

Kirkland was also thankful for the opportunity to
work with a dancer from whom she could gain great
inspiration and knowledge. She says of that time with
Baryshnikov:

> Misha has helped me a lot. He's so devil-may-care. Dancing
> with him is like a conversation. The physicality of dancing
> together is wonderful. But you can't describe how spiritual a
> partnership is. Feelings flow back and forth. Maybe it's
> because we do care about each other, and I not only respond
> to him as a dancer but as a person.

The dancers' relationship quickly became more than
simply a professional one. Soon, Baryshnikov and
Kirkland were virtually inseparable—both on the stage
and off. "I can't help but be a little in love with all my
partners," Misha mused. The Kirkland-Baryshnikov
romance quickly became highly publicized within
dance circles. Audience members too, perhaps, had a
certain fascination with seeing "a couple" perform
together on stage. For the two dancers, it seemed an
ideal match, for they could inspire each other both
emotionally and professionally at the same time.

After his *Giselle* debut at ABT, Baryshnikov entered
a new era in his attitude toward performing. He
appeared now as if he were on fire to dance. It seemed
his new-found freedom and the vast opportunities
open to him caused him to gobble up dance roles with
unheard-of energy. Journalist Stephen Schiff de-
scribed this period:

> What no one anticipated. . . was Misha's hunger. He wanted
> to dance everything, now, and for the next few years he
> performed more roles, and more kinds of roles, than any
> other dancer in memory. . . . At times it seemed he could do
> anything. And would.

Baryshnikov during this period was like a sleek, young, impeccably bred racehorse who had been kept penned up in a small stall for his entire life. Once he was given the freedom to run, he took off at a gallop that never slowed down. "I wanted it badly," remembers Misha. "My years in Russia [were] a bit slow and very frustrating. And the minute I got out, I exploded, because I had so much energy.... I had some kind of anger in me. My body [wanted] to experience everything...."

The reaction to Baryshnikov's defection in the Soviet Union was somewhat odd. The KGB almost never mentioned it, and many members of the Party acted as if it never happened. There was no immediate wave of dismissals at the Kirov or within the Party nor was there a formal demand for excuses or blame. The KGB circulated rumors that Baryshnikov was on an extended professional tour abroad and the date of his return was, at that time, uncertain.

By the fall of 1974, Misha had become close friends with an older Russian emigré named Remi Saunder. Born in Moscow, Saunder had emigrated in the 1930s. Her transition to the West was a difficult one, and one that Baryshnikov could identify with. Saunder's father, who was prevented from leaving the USSR, was later killed in a KGB prison camp. Her understanding of the Russian ex-patriot and her ability to share his pain made her something of a mother figure for Baryshnikov—someone familiar, who replaced a loved one from long ago.

Baryshnikov spent his first months in the United States plunging eagerly into his new culture. Nearly all his spare time was spent at plays, operas, movies, or in front of the television, watching everything from cartoons to the late show. It was rumored that, within weeks, he had already worked up a formidable imitation of Humphrey Bogart.

Baryshnikov (right) danced in Stravinsky's *Petrouchka*, 1977.

His arrival in the United States in the mid-1970s spotlighted—and to some extent caused—an astonishing growth in the popularity of American dance. In 1965, the size of the U.S. dance audience was about 1 million; by 1975 it was estimated at 15 million. During the 1960s, ballet was centered in New York City. By 1975, more than 80 percent of the dance audience, and two dozen companies, were spread all across America—in cities such as Boston, Atlanta, Philadelphia, Pittsburgh, Akron, Sacramento, Chicago, and Los Angeles.

It was no coincidence that the demand for tickets at the ABT box office skyrocketed upon Baryshnikov's arrival, which helped the company financially. In fact, just a few months after he arrived, ABT announced its plan to buy the old Manhattan Opera House for $10 million, fulfilling the dream of the sixty-eight-year-old founder, Lucia Chase, to have a permanent home for ABT in New York City.

With a growing foundation of new friends and a thrilling professional acceptance in the West, Baryshnikov's transition seemed to be going quite well. But an American Ballet Theatre tour to Sydney, Australia, in 1975 would temporarily bring his good fortune to a halt. During a performance of *Don Quixote* at the Sydney Opera House, his ankle buckled, seriously spraining his left foot. The accident had happened after one of Baryshnikov's thrilling high leaps, the landing from which left him in intense pain. Despite his agony, Misha improvised a few steps and reversed some of the choreography so he could favor his right foot. Once his combinations were over, he stood frozen for his two curtain calls, waited for the curtain to fall, and then fainted. It took five weeks of rest, swimming, and Jacuzzi baths to get the dancer back on his feet.

Upon recovery, Misha again tore into his dancing with great enthusiasm. He added nearly twenty new ballets to his repertoire in the space of a year. The total count, from 1974 to 1976, was, as Baryshnikov himself recalled, "twenty-six roles within two years. Not bad for a beginning. In Russia such an achievement would cover my entire artistic life." With that same energy and drive, Misha went on to dance another twenty-two roles with ABT in the following fifteen months. When asked, Baryshnikov would not openly say that all this enthusiasm sprang only from his pure love of his art form. Often, his feelings about dance were much less romantic. "It's my work," he admits, "I have my work . . . and I have my life, the two are completely different." (Baryshnikov often makes this distinction because he considers his private life to be very personal and often refuses to discuss matters of family or friends with anyone. His dancing, or his "work," however, is very public, and it puts him in the public eye, which makes him uncomfortable.) Much of his drive to accomplish so much in so little time came from his unyielding commitment to stretching and challenging his abilities. His steel-coated discipline and his strong competitive nature also motivated him to maintain such a fast pace.

Baryshnikov's involvement with American dance also changed his approach to the art form. The more he studied in the West, the less attached he became to the Soviet dance heritage of "dance-drama," which was most concerned with "telling a story" in dance. Now Baryshnikov favored a more expressive, intellectual, and psychological approach to his roles. This Western trend emphasized dance as an abstract expression of emotion rather than a traditional representational one.

But the American approach did not come easily to the classically trained dancer. For Baryshnikov, it had been unnecessary to find "an emotion" deep within himself to dance a character. He had been taught that ballet is *high art*, to be performed with the utmost excellence, for its beauty springs from its perfection of technique. Every performance was another test of mastery for the dancer, another celebration of internal control and precision. Not much energy was spent reacting to a partner, or to the natural and subtle differences that composed each performance. Baryshnikov recalls dancing *Giselle* with Natalia Makarova once they were reunited in America:

> [We had] already danced *Giselle* so many times that for me each new performance [was] a special sort of recollection. The body's memory almost subconsciously draws out of somewhere new nuances, which in essence are not really new at all. They have already been done.

This idea of the body "having memory" or an "instinct" is one that Baryshnikov explored more in the mid to late 1970s. He began to rely less on the Soviet "presentational" style, which is based on artificial characterizations. He turned, instead, to a more instinctive approach in which the body moved more as though it were on automatic pilot. Movement and dance details were incorporated more spontaneously. This organic style, Baryshnikov thought, would appear more natural and would be better suited to a more honest interpretation on stage.

A ballet entitled *Le Jeune Homme et la Mort (The Young Man and Death)* gave Baryshnikov a unique opportunity to explore this new direction. His involvement enabled him to work with his old friend Roland Petit in this ballet, a work for which famous director and artist Jean Cocteau wrote the story. Misha knew of the reputation Cocteau had as an avant-garde artist and was intrigued by the possibilities of dancing in the production.

Le Jeune Homme et la Mort was first performed in 1946, and was then revived in 1975 by the American Ballet Theatre, especially for Baryshnikov. Petit's demanding choreography evolved during the rehearsal process, as many of the original steps were adapted to fit Misha's incredible ability. Although the production was a creative risk for Misha, the choreography was indeed bold and innovative, and he remained committed to the process for the sake of experimentation. Even if the ballet was flawed, its intellectual ideas and its offbeat dance steps took the dancer in a new direction, one that challenged his classical technique and made him adapt. Much of what challenged him was the choreographer's ability to push him beyond his technique; by taking his physical ability for granted, he was able to respond to the emotion of what was happening on stage. Baryshnikov responded to this new view of dance wholeheartedly:

> Many dancers have fantastic technique. I used to see such fantastic dancers in class. On stage, [just] technique is nakedness. A dancer must learn how to clothe himself. He must know what to wear emotionally in every ballet and how to change from step to step.

Twyla Tharp, celebrated American choreographer, offered Misha a chance in 1976 to continue his quest for abstract roles. She was putting together a production, entitled *Push Comes to Shove,* that would be an irreverent mix of new choreography that poked fun at many of the trappings of classical ballet. The movements and steps exaggerated traditional ballet movement, portraying it as over-contrived, unnecessarily complex, and inaccessible to the general public. For the choreography, Tharp took classical movements and made them disjointed, out of time with the music. She also added completely new movements—shoulder shrugs, muscle contractions, grimaces (exaggerated faces) and bumps (heavy, quick body movements). The synthesis of classical and popular art was a perfect combination for Baryshnikov at this point in his career. Not only did the dancing both require and stretch his classical training, it also pointed out the somewhat stagnant nature of traditional ballet—a sentiment the dancer himself was holding at the time.

Push Comes to Shove also provided a vital breath of fresh air for the dancer at a time when he craved a break from his regular routines. The dance allowed

In 1976, Baryshnikov starred in Twyla Tharp's satirical spoof of classical ballet, *Push Comes to Shove*.

Baryshnikov, shown here in a scene with Leslie Browne, won an Oscar nomination for his portrayal of a playboy-dancer in *The Turning Point*, 1977.

him to show off his great talent for physical comedy as well as his genius for improvisation. Most of all, it offered him a rare opportunity to really *have fun* as he danced.

His involvement with Twyla Tharp encouraged Baryshnikov to continue to explore new ways of using his talent. It was soon after *Push* ended that he was offered a role in Herbert Ross's movie *The Turning Point*. Many who saw the film believed Baryshnikov's character to be an accurate reflection of his real personality. In the movie, he plays a conceited and immoral playboy who treats women poorly. In fact, this character is quite different from the real Baryshnikov. Most people who know him well agree that he is essentially a private person who prefers the company of a few friends to jet-setting around the world. Though he has had a number of relationships with women, many shortlived, much of their failure has been due to his hectic lifestyle, involving a great deal of travel, and his basic hesitance to become permanently committed to someone.

The Turning Point, which tells the story of two rival dancers, was not a pleasant experience for Misha. He thought the plot was contrived, and the movie, overall, mediocre. Nevertheless, his performance in the film was highly praised and won him an Academy Award nomination for Best Supporting Actor in 1977. As always, the dancer proved to himself that if he was willing to extend his talent to unknown areas, he would find almost no boundaries to constrain him.

Baryshnikov danced *Don Quixote* with Gelsey Kirkland for the ABT.

CHAPTER 7

A MASTER'S
PAS DE DEUX

I didn't expect to find a land of milk and honey. I began by dancing Giselle *and things I knew in order to show what I can do. But already there have been new challenges in ballets like Balanchine's* Theme and Variations *and Petit's* Le Jeune Homme et la Mort, *styles I never tried before. What's important to me is not the immediate, but my evolution as a dancer. The life of a dancer burns quickly like a candle. What have I got, six or seven years to dance? I want to fill them. The most terrifying experience must be for a 40-year-old dancer to look back and feel that he did not fulfill himself.*
—Mikhail Baryshnikov

The thought of choreographing a ballet had appealed to Baryshnikov for some time, though he never truly considered himself a choreographer. When the opportunity arose at ABT to do *The Nutcracker*, Misha grabbed the chance. The ballet's premiere, in December of 1976 at the Kennedy Center in Washington, D.C., was a respectable success.

Misha's second effort, which closely followed his first, was *Don Quixote*. With this work, Baryshnikov attempted a more creative and unusual interpretation, leaving many critics and peers dissatisfied with its lack of tradition. The premiere of *Don Quixote*, also at the Kennedy Center but in March of 1978, was

more openly criticized for its shortcomings than
The Nutcracker. It seemed that most people wanted
Baryshnikov to stick with tradition in his approach,
but traditional ideas were not the ones that inspired
him. For the time being, the great dancer would
concentrate on dancing alone. His work as a choreographer was, as he put it, an "experiment"—one that
did not necessarily lead him to more work as a choreographer or director.

In the spring of 1978, Baryshnikov shocked the ballet
world with a defection of a somewhat different sort.
The superstar of the ABT announced he was leaving
the company to join the New York City Ballet (NYCB),
under the direction of the legendary George Balanchine. The ABT troupe was stunned. Not only were
they losing the most talented male dancer in the world
(and a great box-office phenomenon), they were losing
him to their rival company.

Gelsey Kirkland was also losing Misha with this
move. Though their relationship had been rapidly
deteriorating over the past year or two, strained emotions between them probably played only a minor role
in Misha's decision to leave ABT. The years of being
in the public spotlight, as well as their being forced to
work together even during emotionally difficult times,
had finally taken its toll. There were enormous pressures on both dancers to remain successful, not only
romantically but also professionally. These pressures
came from friends and colleagues who enjoyed the
exciting fruits of the couple's collaborations on stage.
It was true, too, that Kirkland had become increasingly
dependent on Misha and had been demanding more
and more of his time and energy. For him, the romance had become more than he was ready for.

Unable to make a longstanding commitment to a
woman who wanted more stability from him,

George Balanchine developed an athletic American style of ballet at the New York City Ballet.

Baryshnikov's move to Balanchine's company put a formal end to whatever relationship was left between him and Kirkland. "I stay committed when the emotional side of the relationship is still at a high level," Misha explains. "If it's dropping down, there's no commitment, because it's torture for both partners. I don't believe in working on relationships. It's nonsense."

Without a doubt, Baryshnikov's prime motivation for making the move was a selfish one: he wanted to work with the seventy-five-year-old Balanchine before it was too late. There was also some amount of pressure from leaders in the ballet world who didn't want to see two of the greatest talents of the twentieth century waste an opportunity to collaborate. Baryshnikov said about Balanchine when his announcement was made, "I would love to be an instrument in his wonderful hands. . . . The repertory of the New York City Ballet is enormous. I have so many opportunities to try myself out. . . . Slowly I realized that I would never forgive myself if I did not try. I am thirty, with a few years left."

Balanchine was idolized as one of the fathers of American dance. He had singlehandedly created a new style of dancing—less classical and more athletic and abstract—and had pioneered some of the most innovative and unique choreography in the world. Balanchine has been credited for the blossoming of dance that took place in America in the 1970s. Not only was his choreography a bold and exciting departure from anything the dance world had previously seen, he was incredibly prolific. And his influence spread quickly. More than twenty U.S. dance companies relied on his original ballets for the foundations of their repertories in the 1970s. Today, even more dance companies across the country stage Balanchine ballets.

The Balanchine style has been one of the greatest influences on the direction of modern ballet in America. His choreography changed the nature of ballet by making movement less tied to storytelling and more dependent upon music. The complexity of his music forced him to stretch the potential of the human body in his choreography and to constantly create original movements that would make the notes visible and his dance felt.

Balanchine's style was vastly different from the style Baryshnikov had already mastered. It would require Misha to learn an entirely new set of movements, to use his muscles in a way foreign to his Soviet training, and to express the emotions of the ballets in a completely different style. Though he had begun to explore this demanding style when he worked with Twyla Tharp, Balanchine's choreography was even more rigorous and athletic in an off-centered way. The constant performance of such movements also required a much more thorough training than was required for the few individual roles Baryshnikov had danced for Tharp.

There were many people who originally doubted Baryshnikov's ability to adapt to such a new world successfully. But clearly, that was exactly the challenge the dancer craved. As Gennady Smakov phrased it in his book *Baryshnikov,* "In tackling Balanchine, Misha had to struggle against the Russian way of performing, which practically ran in his blood. To a certain degree it was supposed to be the last hard blow by Baryshnikov against himself—his image of the Russian virtuoso, his theatrical instincts and devices." Balanchine, too, must have recognized how difficult it would be for a Soviet-trained dancer to learn his choreography. A Soviet dancer had never been accepted into the ranks of the NYCB—and that included such superstars as Nureyev and Makarova. Baryshnikov's abilities, however, were great enough to persuade the NYCB director to break precedent just this once.

The move to the NYCB meant many sacrifices other than those involved in retraining for a completely new style of dance. For one thing, Misha would no longer receive the average $3,500 per performance he earned at ABT, but would be paid a standard $750 per week salary. Balanchine detested the "star system" so common in other companies around the world. Accordingly, the NYCB was run on an everyone-as-equals basis, and the Soviet superstar would be no exception. The director was also known as a man who demanded total control of his dancers—both on stage and off—and needed to have the utmost dedication and obedience from his subjects so that he could mold them into his visions on the stage. Balanchine would often become involved in the private lives of his troupe members, telling them how to dress and who to see. Baryshnikov recalls that Balanchine, "taught his ballerinas what to wear, what kind of perfume to use, what kind of hairdo to have, what jewelry to wear. . . . He conducted every moment of their lives." It was all part of Balanchine's dedication to creating "total dancers," a style of management to which Misha was certainly not accustomed. Still, these circumstances did not lessen Baryshnikov's determination to join the company. It was obvious that his insatiable drive to grow artistically and to find new challenges made any sacrifices worthwhile. Baryshnikov explained, "I did not come to the States to make money. It's a good thing, but not the main one. . . . As for my superstar position, it really doesn't mean very much to me. Celebrity is like having extra sugar in your coffee."

Under Balanchine, Baryshnikov was bombarded with challenges and new directions each day. This new routine seemed to be exactly what he needed at this point in his career, when he was feeling he had reached an artistic and technical dead end. Now, the dancer felt he was becoming more expressive as he learned to understand dance in a whole new light. "There can be no comparison between a Baryshnikov and a Balanchine dancer such as Villella," wrote Hubert Saal. "The Russian's whole life has been devoted to acquiring the technique needed to dance a handful of romantic ballets. Balanchine incessantly invents new technical demands for his dancers."

The sharp, stop-and-go style of Balanchine's chore-ography was particularly hard for Baryshnikov to master. The new combinations, twists, jumps, and turns put a great strain on a body that had, for so long, become comfortable with grand, smooth, majestic movements. Yet, this experience renewed his enthusi-asm and expanded his repertoire beyond that of any male dancer who had ever come before him.

Balanchine's athletic, concentrated movements now created the basis of Misha's repertoire. The movements were expressions that were not meant primarily to tell a story or to be filled with a great emotional message. The beauty would come in the movement itself rather than the perfect execution of classic steps. This idea of focusing on the "pure" expressiveness of the movement is what Balanchine called the "disinterested beauty" of his style. He wanted his dance to seem like an abstract painting in motion rather than a realistic painting in motion. He wanted to strive for pure dancing that was not bogged down with any message.

Balanchine, who had studied classical ballet in the Soviet Union, drew on the steps of Russian ballet as one of his foundations. At the same time, he did away largely with the old convention of storytelling and added other influences, such as jazz, tap, and Broadway styles, to keep his choreography fresh and unpredictable. Balanchine rejected the notion that dance was a predictable series of combinations and preparations with clear beginnings and ends. Instead, he blended movement in one long, interlocked stream of swift, dense, continuous motion. In this way, dance at the New York City Ballet was not made up of blocks of interrelated movement that formed a whole dance; it was instead a continuous flow of unbroken move-ment.

Not everyone in the world of dance was convinced that Balanchine was perfect. The European dance critics, in particular, criticized the choreographer for what they saw as a lack of classical attention. The Europeans disliked the "look" of Balanchine, which focused a great deal on the feet.

As with any art form that goes against the established traditions, there will be those who disapprove and find fault. Yet, the fact remains that George Balanchine and his NYCB troupe were exploring new territories that opened up the possibilities of modern ballet to infinite variation. For that great contribution, some failures and shortcomings are surely acceptable.

For twelve months, Baryshnikov worked with his new teacher, rehearsing up to fifteen ballets at once. On November 14, 1978, the NYCB opened its season with *Rubies,* a production in which Baryshnikov's talents were shown off. After a few other ballets, Balanchine mounted a revival of his masterpiece, *The Prodigal Son,* which challenged his Soviet dancer more than he had ever been challenged before. Then came three classics for children, *The Nutcracker, Harlequinade,* and *The Steadfast Tin Soldier,* all of which made conservative use of Baryshnikov's abilities. Balanchine created no new works specifically for Misha.

After a while, Misha began to feel stifled, convinced that his full potential was not being tapped, and his distress showed through to the critics. Many dance writers began to notice that Baryshnikov did not seem happy. The suggestion that the collaboration might not be right rang truer and truer each day. Although Balanchine's choreography was fascinating, it did not seem to properly utilize the truest talents of a perfect classical dancer.

In *Symphony in C, Donizetti Variations,* and *The Four Temperaments,* it appeared more obvious to those who

George Balanchine directed Baryshnikov in the production of *The Prodigal Son* with the New York City Ballet.

had followed Misha's career that he was not dancing his best. At times he would even give an "off" performance—expected from most dancers but never from Baryshnikov. These problems did not point to a deficiency in the dancer's technique, only to the fact that he was dancing roles for which he could never be suited. The speed required by Balanchine's choreography allowed no time for classical set ups. These are movements that prepare a dancer for a particular step, like a *grand jeté*. The lack of preparation made the perfection of each step impossible. The pace and

Four legends of twentieth-century dance assembled in 1987 for the ABT's annual choreography workshop. From left to right, Agnes de Mille, Baryshnikov, Jerome Robbins, and Paul Taylor.

rhythm of the music demanded a kind of response that went squarely against all that felt natural to Misha.

While still at the NYCB, Baryshnikov performed in the work of dance genius Jerome Robbins, whose *Other Dances* had been choreographed especially for Misha in 1976 (while he was still with ABT). The production was a smash success for Baryshnikov, who felt his brilliance return as he danced with his partner Patricia McBride. Robbins's choreographic style was more compatible with Soviet classical ballet and the fact that the dancing was devised specifically with Baryshnikov in mind made a world of difference. As appealing as the "everyone-as-equals" notion may have been, it seemed inevitable that Misha would shine his brightest as a star.

Baryshnikov's last appearance with the NYCB was as a poet in *La Sonnambula* on October 12, 1979, at the Kennedy Center. After that production, the dancer resigned from the company citing tendonitis and other injuries as his primary reasons for leaving. The Balanchine repertoire had, of course, taken a great toll on Baryshnikov's body, one that he only intensified with his unyielding drive to master such an alien style. But there were other reasons Misha decided it was time to depart. In June, 1979, an unexpected offer from the ABT invited him to become artistic director of the company beginning in 1980. It seemed a perfect opportunity for the dancer to make a move and, perhaps, to lessen his pace of dancing and ease into other areas. After all, from July 1978 to October 1979, he had performed twenty-two new roles with the NYCB and, even though his tenure with Balanchine had mixed results, Baryshnikov had accomplished much of what he wished:

> You get good notices, you become successful, you become accustomed to something, and you are comfortable. But dancers have to be mad and hungry. Balanchine was wonderful, a challenge. . . . I'll never regret that I worked with him. He is a great man and a great choreographer. And I think he deflated certain of my fantasies about myself while helping me to acquire greater confidence in my field.

Baryshnikov had taken on the greatest challenge of his career; he had taken chances and explored risks that no other dancer had ever attempted. And, though he had met with some failure, he knew the past year had strengthened his technique enormously and that even with failure comes a valuable broadening of knowledge.

In his television special, *Baryshnikov on Broadway*, Misha danced with Liza Minnelli.

CHAPTER 8

WARMING UP THE ABT

He expected all of us to be the best, 100 percent, all the time.
I remember the mazurka rehearsals, when he would show a step
and it would give you the feeling inside that you needed to do
it correctly. He was especially wonderful in the character
dances, which are dependent on feeling
rather than just technique.
—Lillie Stewart, ABT dancer

In between his leaving the NYCB and his becoming artistic director of the ABT, Baryshnikov kept himself quite busy. Before completing a series of trips to Buenos Aires, London, and Paris, the dancer received an honorary Doctorate of Fine Arts from Yale University and then flew to China to appear in a Bob Hope television special for which he danced the second act of *Giselle.* Then, after a vacation in the Caribbean, Misha agreed to appear in a television special of his own, entitled *Baryshnikov on Broadway,* in which he would salute the American musical theater. His one specific request for the special was that he would be able to work with Liza Minnelli, whose talent as a singer, dancer, and actress Baryshnikov greatly admired.

Much of Misha's love for Broadway went back to his lifetime fascination with America's classic movies, where tough guys—James Cagney in particular—could dance and still be tough. The diversity that Cagney showed in his films—a romantic singer-dancer in one, then a cold-blooded killer in the next—inspired the young Russian dancer. "In a funny way," Baryshnikov once said, "[Cagney] was one of the first big influences on me."

For his special, Baryshnikov studied tap dancing, a style of dance he found difficult to master. Tap requires a "very sharp control." The dancer has to isolate small areas of the body. While the legs and feet are sharply controlled with tiny movements, the upper body is often left loose and relaxed in tap, which requires the dancer to be both fluid and rigid at the

To prepare for *Baryshnikov on Broadway*, Misha worked with Michael Bennett, author and choreographer for *A Chorus Line* .

same time—a completely foreign concept to a classic ballet dancer.

The premiere of *Baryshnikov on Broadway*, which aired on April 24, 1980, both excited and disappointed many of the dancer's fans. For those who enjoy seeing Misha experiment with his art, the special was an endearing blend of classical dance technique with American stylings. Those who frown upon what they consider to be an inferior dance medium felt the great ballet virtuoso was wasting his talent. They did not care that the superstar was, indeed, having fun.

Baryshnikov was having fun in other areas of his life as well. His recent involvement in Hollywood and television projects had introduced him to many new friends in the entertainment industry. Sometime between 1979 and 1980, at a party given by actor Buck Henry, Misha met a beautiful young actress named Jessica Lange. Film director Milos Forman introduced the couple who, according to Baryshnikov, fell in love at first sight. It was at this point that a somewhat tumultuous love affair began between the dancer and the actress.

Throughout their more than five years together, the demands of complex careers and their very different emotional needs would cause them great turmoil. At first, the greatest strain was the fact that Baryshnikov was already an established international star while Lange was only just beginning to become known. (While he was doing *Baryshnikov on Broadway*, she was playing the helpless victim captured by King Kong in Dino de Laurentis's movie version of the well-known ape thriller.) Both Lange and Misha were constantly distracted from their relationship by the intense demands of their careers. Lange was overwhelmed and obsessed with "inventing herself" and her public persona during this time, and often had little energy left for personal conflicts. Baryshnikov was in great demand both as a dancer and as an actor, and was pursuing a number of major projects that were key to his career. The two would go for weeks without seeing each other, and neither was much good at phone relationships.

The second greatest strain on the dancer and the actress was the difference between them in the way they communicated their feelings to each other. "Their relationship was very, very volatile," one friend re-members. "Misha wasn't used to the psychiatric way that people like [Jessica] speak to each other—'Why don't you get into your feelings and get over it'—you know." Many observers also felt that Lange was not able to share Misha's sense of humor, that she was often very serious and very tough on everyone around her—including herself. "Misha is a stitch and a card," a friend says. "One thing Jessica Lange could never be is a card." Despite the emotional storms, they pro-duced a child in 1981—a daughter named Alexandra, after Misha's mother.

In addition to his new personal commitments, Misha had also taken on an enormous task at the American Ballet Theatre in New York. When Baryshnikov took the helm at ABT in September 1980, his new responsibility filled many with doubts and fear that he could not handle the job. At thirty-two years of age, with no previous experience, Misha was taking over the job from the seventy-three-year-old Lucia Chase, who had run the company with Oliver Smith for more than thirty-five years. He was also inheriting a ninety-member troupe of dancers with a repertoire of over seventy-five ballets, a $10 million annual budget, and a past history of serious financial deficits. Under the new policy, fortunately, the artistic director would not have to worry about ABT's money

The romantic relationship of Misha and Jessica Lange was stormy and emotionally demanding. The couple did have a daughter together, Alexandra.

problems. That, they said, would be left to Chairman Donald M. Kendall (also chairman of Pepsico) and executive director Herman Krawitz. Aside from his youth, people worried about the fact that Misha had never before managed anything, much less a large, complicated, and taxing organization like ABT. Those people, however, did not realize that they now had an artistic director who thrived on impossible challenges just like this one.

Some critics complained that Baryshnikov would "Russify" a great American ballet company. In fact, Baryshnikov did employ many of the classical Soviet techniques to train his dancers, but he was also dedicated to preserving the company's distinctly American flavor. He wanted to upgrade the quality of the entire company while still reflecting all the major trends in dance that were evolving. Deborah Trustman of *The New York Times* wrote,

> Establishing continuity is Baryshnikov's aim. In the Russian tradition, he wants his young American dancers to understand that dance is more than movement. It is the physical expression of emotion. Above all, it is theater: every step, every expression, must contribute to the magical illusion on stage, which he calls the "beautiful lie."

A well-rounded repertoire, balanced between classical and modern, was the goal Baryshnikov hoped to eventually achieve for his company. For his first year, he focused on classics, such as *Swan Lake* and *Sleeping Beauty*.

Despite all the doubts from the ABT community, Baryshnikov began his work with a serious purpose and great resolve—just as he had as a dancer from the very beginning. One of his first actions was the cancellation of ABT's fall season, which he replaced with a rigorous and unprecedented thirteen-week rehearsal schedule. He insisted that all members of the company take a class every day to study acting and mime techniques as well as literature, and he let his principal dancers know that he intended to restructure the ABT soloist and casting system along the lines of Balanchine's New York City Ballet. There were no pre-determined stars of the company. Instead, Baryshnikov wanted to promote dancers from within the company, something Lucia Chase did not do. One dancer said at the time, "Nobody really knew where they stood under Lucia. Now they are more secure— and also more angry."

Other significant changes included computerizing rehearsal schedules, reworking many of ABT's classic ballets, and firing the company's most visible star, ex-girlfriend Gelsey Kirkland, because her increasing drug use caused her performance and her personality to become erratic and unpredictable. Previously, principal dancers were paid on a per-performance basis, but Baryshnikov wanted them more available. He offered his dancers a straight salary (in the Balanchine style) with a season contract, which decreased many dancers' incomes but made their lives more stable. Most dancers were reluctant but went along.

"When he got there," ABT choreographer and friend Peter Anastos said, "American Ballet Theater was dominated by a flimsy star system. There was no *corps de ballet* to speak of, and the company could not mount a ballet where scenery, costumes, music, dancing, and production really added up." Many dancers were dismissed, others were constantly neglected. Baryshnikov made it clear that any dancer in the company, regardless of current status, could be in line for solo or principal roles if they worked hard enough.

Whether or not Baryshnikov's tough policies were popular or not, the ABT troupe was sure of one thing: their director was dedicated to being involved on every level. Misha's role was indeed unique in the history of ABT, for he was not only the manager, he was a dancer as well. During the first few years, he attended all classes and rehearsals and worked very closely with the company. He performed in many productions and was much more a part of the company than any director had ever been. Lisa de Ribere, a dancer with ABT, says of Baryshnikov's influence,

> Working with Misha is different from working with Balanchine. Misha is a dancer as opposed to a choreographer. I think the unique thing about him is that he's there with us every day, taking classes with us, dancing the same ballets with us, rehearsing—I mean, he's sweating as much, or more, than any of us. And he's a fantastic example. Anything we can do, he can do better!

By the end of his first year as artistic director, Baryshnikov's positive example was evident in the quality of ABT dance. Chief dance critic for *The New York Times*, Anna Kisselgoff, wrote at the opening of Misha's first season, "The dancers have been fantastically rehearsed and this has been immediately visible in the discipline, vitality, and new precision of the corps."

Other public reaction to ABT's first season under Baryshnikov was mixed. Some people criticized Baryshnikov for "training his dancers in public," by using his young, exciting, yet not as polished performers for many classic roles. But the director was firm in his policy and once told an interviewer, "Audiences don't care who they see in new ballets, it should be the same for the classics." Other criticism came from audiences that did not appreciate the many "plotless ballets" the company performed. Responding to this, Baryshnikov added Roland Petit's *Carmen* to the 1982 season, along with *Billy the Kid* and *Pillar of Fire*. But, staying true to his vision about new works and promising talents, Misha also commissioned a new ballet from Singapore-born choreographer Choo San Goh, called *Configurations.* In it he used several promising dancers from the *corps de ballet*, emphasizing his no-star system and his dedication to using soloists only if they were right. The tour that year was the most successful in the company's history.

In Chicago, during a 1982 rehearsal, Baryshnikov suffered a knee injury that kept him off his feet for about six months. Though he was upset by his immobility, it was interesting for those around him to see how relaxed and calm he was about the situation. Misha recalled, "I once said to somebody that I take my vacations when I am injured. That's when I lie on the beach. It's very interesting psychologically—whether I use injuries to relieve the pressure."

Indeed, he had been going almost nonstop as the new head of ABT for nearly two years straight. His high-pressure position left him little time to take a breath. Much of that pressure, according to Misha's close friend, poet Joseph Brodsky, comes from an incredible drive within. Brodsky says that much of Baryshnikov's drive comes from his unusual intelligence. "He is a dancer, he is not supposed to be intelligent. He is too intelligent for his medium." It is that intelligence and curiosity that keeps Baryshnikov in constant search for new dances, new experiences, new teachers, and new challenges.

In 1983, Baryshnikov came under fire for spending too much time on his extracurricular projects and not enough time with his ballet company. This criticism, combined with recent problems of dancers' strikes and a $2 million budget deficit on the ABT books, prompted Misha to submit his resignation to the board of directors. The board did not accept it. Instead, the artistic director agreed to stay on the condition that he be paid only a dollar per year, that he be allowed to spend less time on fundraising activities, and that his directorship be evaluated without regard to his personal career endeavors.

Baryshnikov promptly went to work on ABT's grand new 1984 production of *Cinderella*, co-choreographed with Peter Anastos. The ballet would be the first full-evening production ever mounted by the company and would also turn out to be the most expensive in the history of ABT (costs exceeded $1 million). Though the show did exceptionally well at the box office, it did poorly where Misha most wanted to succeed. The critics, by and large, hated it. Arlene Croce of *The New Yorker* wrote after the premiere of *Cinderella* that it was "still very much a work in progress," and continued by blasting both the set designer and the lighting designer for their misguided visions of the fairy tale. Other critics scolded Baryshnikov for over-intellectualizing the story, in essence, taking the magic out of it and turning it into a "heartless burlesque."

Baryshnikov's response to the critics was typically guarded, yet in keeping with his philosophy about dance and his own career: "I am not interested in whether the ballets are good or not. When you ask a choreographer to make a ballet, you can't guarantee that it's going to be good. . . . The important thing is that we do it."

Misha rehearses *Cinderella* with Kevin McKenzie and Cynthia Harvey.

Financial cutbacks and debts plagued the beginning of the spring 1984 season at ABT. Baryshnikov decided to produce Kenneth MacMillan's *Romeo and Juliet*, a ballet that offered his dancers juicy roles for the soloists and plenty of plot. This time his judgement was also critically well-received and rewarded with a successful box office that took some of the financial pressure off the company.

Another film project presented itself in 1984, enabling Baryshnikov to once again combine his two great loves—dancing and acting. The movie, *White Nights*, starred Misha, tap dancer Gregory Hines, and Isabella Rossellini. The movie was directed by the commercially successful Hollywood director Taylor Hackford.

The story line of *White Nights* was very similar in many ways to Baryshnikov's life. It is about a world-famous Russian dancer (Baryshnikov) who defects from the Soviet Union and becomes a big star in America. Later, at the height of his success in the West, his plane needs to make an emergency landing in Siberia, en route to Tokyo. The dancer-defector is then held as a captive of the country he had left, where he is considered a criminal. While there, he meets a black tap dancer from New York who had defected to Russia. The two eventually help each other to regain their freedom by making a daring escape to the American embassy in Moscow. The movie opens with ten minutes of Baryshnikov performing the end of Roland Petit's classic *Le Jeune Homme et la Mort*. Other choreography, mostly the tap dancing sequences between Hines and Baryshnikov, was done by long-time friend and colleague Twyla Tharp.

In addition to being Misha's greatest acting challenge on film to date, he was again confronted with having to tap dance. After he finished work on the

Baryshnikov with his co-stars in the film, *White Nights*, Isabella Rossellini and Gregory Hines.

picture, Baryshnikov admitted that, of all the dancing styles he has had to master through the years, the tap dancing he had to learn for *White Nights* and for his television special *Baryshnikov on Broadway* presented the greatest problem for him. "Just forget it," the dancer remembers, "I tried very hard when Gregory Hines gave me pointers, but I was the dumbest. My legs wouldn't work that way."

The critics, however, who praised his acting in the film, didn't seem to notice many flaws in

Baryshnikov's performance when the film opened in 1985. *Vogue* film critic Molly Haskell wrote:

> *White Nights* proves that Baryshnikov is not only our most glorious dancer, he could be our greatest movie actor, given half a chance. . . . His command of space is absolute. He is stillness itself, and then, with no perceptible transition, he is violent motion. He defies gravity and time, defines beauty as a state of perpetual fluidity, which is one of the things that movies are all about.

Though the film itself received lukewarm reviews from movie writers, *White Nights* was a satisfying commercial success. The film also made Baryshnikov more than just a ballet dancer to millions of Americans; it launched him into the realm of movie star and matinee idol and made him one of Hollywood's hottest new properties.

It is possible that the many pressures of his new-found commercial success complicated Misha's personal life. His longstanding romance with Jessica Lange formally ended in 1985, when, according to many reports, she left him. It seemed their already volatile relationship could not sustain the great amounts of time away from each other that acting and dancing careers demanded. Neither could it sustain the news that Misha had been—and still was—romantically involved with ABT ballerina Lisa Rinehart during his relationship with Lange.

The failure of his romance with Lange had a devastating effect on Misha. According to friends, it was the only relationship that ever crushed him when it ended. When he is asked about the greatest disappointments in his life, Baryshnikov invariably includes his breakup with Lange at the top of the list. "Yes, I regret that my relationship with Jessie didn't work out the way we'd wanted and had planned," Misha admits. "It's a big regret that will be there for the rest of my

life. She was—and always will be—one of the very
few women I have loved in my life."

By October of 1986, Baryshnikov tried to take his
mind off of his personal problems by staying hard at
work in Italy on his next film, entitled *Dancers*. Directed by Herbert Ross (who directed *The Turning
Point*), the new movie told the story of a ballet company that undertakes to make a film version of *Giselle*.
As they work on their project, the "real lives" of the
company's members begin to mirror those of the
characters in *Giselle*. The two lead characters become
entangled in a web of jealousy, pain, and betrayal that
resolves itself in much the same way as the classic
ballet they are performing.

Even with his success as a box-office draw,
Baryshnikov is still uncomfortable calling himself a
serious actor. Some of his uneasiness stems from his
strong critical nature, which makes him feel less sure
of his ability when he is doing something other than
dancing. Asked about his second career, he just
shrugs and says, "It's like when you buy a used car.
'Well,' people tell you, 'for a third car it's okay.' Well,
for a second career, this [acting] is fine."

Director Herbert Ross's explanation sheds some
more light on why Baryshnikov may feel uncomfortable:

> Dancers are not used to expressing a dramatic idea verbally.
> They want to externalize everything, which leads to a kind of
> falsity, and they recognize this. The difference between
> actors and dancers is that actors have a technique to internal-
> ize emotion and recreate it; dancers don't. They operate on
> instinct.

Given this, Baryshnikov's success in movies is even
more of an achievement. As a classically trained
Soviet dancer, he has had to work hard to translate his
emotions to a screen where sadness can be expressed

by one tear falling down a cheek in an extreme close-up, unlike the grand gesture of pain on stage.

Once his work on *Dancers* was complete, Misha yearned to return to the stage. He spent much of 1987 involved in a dizzying schedule that would have retired most thirty-nine-year-olds for good. Among his many endeavors that year was a thirty-five-city tour with *Baryshnikov and Company*, where he and ten ballerinas played to sellout crowds of up to 15,000 across the country. After the tour, he helped the dance community raise $1.4 million for AIDS by appearing in and organizing a benefit performance, entitled *Dancing for Life*, that put thirteen major dance companies together at Lincoln Center. Misha was the host, featured artist, and the chief box-office draw for an audience that was for the most part not die-hard ballet fans.

The night after the benefit, Misha was back onstage with Rudolf Nureyev in a production by the Martha Graham Dance Company entitled *Appalachian Spring*, a celebration of American pioneer life. Just a few days later, on October 9, he was attending the premiere of *Dancers* in New York City. (Unfortunately, the film was not met with much enthusiasm and did not stay in theaters very long. It does remain, however, for those who can find it on video, a wonderful opportunity to see Baryshnikov dancing *Giselle*—a part he has perfected to such a degree over the years that it is considered his signature piece.)

Toward the end of 1987, Misha appeared in a PBS television special for the *Dance in America* series. For that program, he performed numerous roles in David Gordon's fantasy ballet entitled *Murder*. Once again, Baryshnikov shone as he played wildly different parts—including a mad scientist and a master spy—and spanned his entire range of emotions, from the comic to the tragic. After his work for PBS,

Baryshnikov rehearses *American Document* under the watchful
gaze of choreographer, Martha Graham.

Baryshnikov set his mind to the upcoming program at his dance company.

ABT's eight-week spring season, April–June of 1988 at the Metropolitan Opera House in New York City, was the most financially successful in Baryshnikov's eight-year tenure. It was also the most popular with audiences and critics alike. Critic Otis Stuart evaluated the 1988 company this way:

> This sleek, streamlined *corps de ballet* . . . is capable of a uniformity and clarity not in the vocabulary of the ABT corps of old. . . . By season's end, these three areas—the corps, the repertoire, and the principal women—had emerged as the most suggestive demarcations of the distance ABT has traveled under Baryshnikov.

The ballet company had collected a record $7 million-plus in ticket sales that season and increased its core audience significantly in the process. Evidently, the mixture of productions and diversity of styles was just what ABT's followers craved. In addition to the usual beloved classics, the new repertoire had included Balanchine ballets that had not been done previously, plus premieres from ABT senior choreographer Agnes de Mille and the newcomer Mark Morris.

Later that year, Misha danced for another *Dance in America* program entitled "Baryshnikov Dances Balanchine with American Ballet Theater." For that production, Baryshnikov danced an old favorite—Balanchine's *Apollo*—in addition to performing a ballet new for him, entitled *Who Cares?* The broadcast, which aired in October of 1988, received the usual mix of reactions. There were mediocre reviews for the company but stellar praise for Baryshnikov. His performance proved that, even as he neared forty, he was not too old or too image-conscious to take on new roles in new ballets.

Baryshnikov and Makarova in the ABT production of *Swan Lake*.

CHAPTER 9

BOWING OUT OF ABT

*I need a new direction in my life. I feel sometimes like
a kind of civil servant. I left one country to be free and
to choose what I want to do, but you run a company
like ABT, there's a lot of obligations which is not
necessarily pleasing obligations. And I would like to
go and explore another world. I was never 100 percent
a ballet person. My friends are usually not ballet
people, you know. It's a bit too narrow for me. And
people who spend all their life with the ballet, they
live day and night in this...soup.*
—Mikhail Baryshnikov

The production of *Swan Lake* that Baryshnikov
was choreographing at the end of 1988 was something
of a dream come true for him. He had longed to stage
a version of the classic since his arrival at ABT in 1980.
Now, finally, the time had come.

Baryshnikov's *Swan Lake* was somewhat untradi-
tional and innovative in its psychological approach to
the characters and staging. Costumes and sets, too,
were a strange blend of the familiar and unknown. It
was clear, however, to all who saw the production that
each deviation from the norm was carefully thought
through by the artistic director.

After its premiere on December 2, 1988, in Costa Mesa, California, the show received controversial reviews from critics across the country. Some critics found the innovative approach refreshing. Others thought Misha had gone too far. By the time *Swan Lake* arrived in New York for the spring 1989 season, there was little waffling by the critics—they hated it. One reviewer wrote that the "quasi-traditionalist interpretation [is] vague, confusing, wrong-headed." Most others agreed that Baryshnikov had bogged down the ballet in heavy and uninviting psychoanalysis.

The disappointment regarding his show was one of the many factors that led to Misha's first announcement of resignation from ABT in June of 1989. *Swan Lake* was a ballet he had felt particularly connected to, one that he thought he understood very deeply, and one in which he invested much of himself. A close associate at the time observed that the reviews were "a disaster psychologically for him. He just didn't know what to do. It was a much bigger disaster than *Cinderella*." Some of his disappointment in the ballet's reception also stemmed from the fact that the world's greatest dancer found it difficult to tolerate failure. Baryshnikov also felt, as he said, that "somehow, the kind of dancing I like, nobody else likes." These feelings, the reviews, and a general weariness of the politics involved in being artistic director all contributed to Misha's decision to resign his post.

There were other troubles that had developed by the spring of 1989 as well. It was during that time that Misha arranged for Jane Hermann to become ABT's new executive director. Hermann was an independent, no-nonsense businesswoman who was known for her hands-on management style. When Baryshnikov initially hired Hermann, he pledged that he would remain with ABT for another three years. A month after the new director arrived, however, Misha had a change of heart and announced he would leave at the end of ABT's 1990 season. His last year with the company, as he planned it then, would be ABT's fiftieth anniversary and would offer him a tailor-made time to help the ballet company celebrate before his exit. But it did not work out that way.

Baryshnikov with daughter Alexandra in 1987.

In 1989, Baryshnikov took on the role of Gregor Samsa, in the stage adaptation of Kafka's classic story of a man changed into an insect, *Metamorphosis*.

A power struggle began brewing that fateful spring. From her first day, Hermann made her two primary objectives clear. The first was to patch up the financial trouble ABT was in, for they were now more than $1 million in debt. Next, she wanted to move ABT's second-in-command, Charles France, out of the way so she could have more absolute power. Hermann demanded that France "take a leave of absence" with full salary and benefits for a year. This power play enraged Misha, and France refused to move. When the board of directors finally backed Hermann's plan, Baryshnikov announced his resignation effective immediately, on September 25. He also insisted that his name be removed from all official documents of ABT without delay.

While *Swan Lake* was in performance and tensions heightened at ABT, Baryshnikov had begun rehearsals for his upcoming Broadway debut as an actor. The show, directed by Steven Berkoff, was *Metamorphosis*. It was based on the 1915 short story by Franz Kafka. The surrealistic work was about a man, Gregor Samsa, who wakes up one morning to find out that he has been transformed into an insect. For Baryshnikov, the acting challenge was both intriguing and clearcut: he would have to act like, and move like, an insect on stage.

Metamorphosis opened in May 1989 to unfavorable reviews that characterized the production as "cartoony" and purposely jarring and disturbing. Nevertheless, Baryshnikov's acting was praised by many who appreciated the demands of such a role. Nancy Vreeland Dalva, a critic for *Dance* magazine and for WNYC-FM in New York, called Misha's acting "extraordinary" and said that he was a "born actor who became the greatest dancer of his day."

As always, the quality of the overall production was of secondary importance. Regardless of its flaws, Baryshnikov managed to shine in his own right, as he had in countless productions in the past. It doesn't seem to matter whether he is part of a smash or a flop, the public is always loyal to him.

Baryshnikov is always on the lookout for new merchandising ventures. Here he introduces his new perfume, 'Misha'.

CONCLUSION

PUSHING IN NEW DIRECTIONS

Baryshnikov is at a crossroads. From the vaulting, elegant creature for whom the air has always seemed as much home as the earth, he has metamorphosed into something new: an actor, an entrepreneur, the Misha of "Misha" perfume, the Baryshnikov of Baryshnikov Bodywear. . . . He is not so much a dancer as the first crossover star in ballet history, a star even bigger than Nijinsky, Pavlova, or Nureyev—the kind of super-idol whose renown extends to those who have never seen him dance, have never seen him act, have never seen him on television.
—Stephen Schiff, *Vanity Fair*, 1989

For Misha, the 1990s will undoubtedly be filled with a surprising collection of new adventures and impressive accomplishments. Already, the dancer has branched out into a number of merchandising efforts for many different markets. His licensing company, Hamilton Projects, has arranged the manufacture and sale of "Baryshnikov Bodywear" and "Misha" perfume. Soon a new line of children's clothing, called "Kids Baryshnikov," will be launched by yet another company. "Baryshnikov Bodywear" had sales of $30 million in 1988 and seems to have done even better for 1989. The perfume, the creation and production of which the dancer supervised from beginning to end, has remained a great success ever since its introduction in June of 1989. Baryshnikov has truly become an American media phenomenon.

Much of the merchandising Baryshnikov has authorized is, according to him, so that he may continue to support the many poor Russian emigrés he funds each year on a personal basis. The dancer, now a multimillionaire, has been known in the past to have given away a good deal of his personal wealth to his compatriots as they struggle to survive in their new country. Friend and poet Joseph Brodsky, who Baryshnikov met just a few weeks after he came to America, says of the dancer, "He helps many people, you know. He finances emigré publications, and he supports people who have come to the United States."

Baryshnikov is not planning to give up dancing entirely, but he does feel ready to focus most of his energies on other pursuits, including giving more time to his personal life. He explains it this way:

> It's a question of stopping dancing, a question of being a man in general. Dancing doesn't excite me the way it used to. I did it all. . . . I still take a ninety-minute class every day; if I miss one day of exercise, I feel I punish my body. But the body memory is stronger than visual memory, and sometimes—in the mirror—you catch yourself pushing in one direction, and you see a reflection of somebody else. Then it's a philosophy of how to age and what to do with it. For instance, I don't have that much elevation now, and I fake some steps because of my physical problems. But I'm a better dancer now—maybe less sensational, maybe less people will be jumping from their chairs—but I am a smarter dancer. I dig into different aspects of dance, which I didn't have a chance to do before.

Though he plans to dance less often, Misha will still continue to do benefits and special projects that interest him. There are a number of dance-related jobs that hold a certain appeal, such as appearing with the celebrated young American choreographer Mark Morris and his dance company.

Other professional plans include a new movie with Gene Hackman (the film is tentatively titled *Dinosaurs*) and exploring more acting roles for Broadway and television.

On a personal level, Misha hopes to spend more time building a stable private life with his longtime friend and companion Lisa Rinehart and their new son, Peter, who was born in July of 1989. Rinehart, according to friends, is perfect for Misha. She is kind, patient, and completely devoted to their life together. One friend says, "Over these years she has sat there and witnessed a lot of infidelities . . . and she's continued to live with him, and now she has his child. . . . She's stood by him. At the house in the country, she's a very quiet presence; she's just there, taking care of him, but not a servant and not a housewife." Somehow, it seems Rinehart has accepted the fact that Misha strains at permanent, confining commitments. Instead of fighting it, she allows him to go about his life as he pleases, confident that he will always return to her when he is really in need.

Misha maintains that he and Jessica Lange now have a good relationship—they are friends—and he is happy with the home Lange and her constant companion Sam Shepard are providing for daughter Alexandra (nicknamed Shura). Lange, Misha, and Alexandra were seen together at the opening of Lange's movie "Men Don't Leave," where they proved to the world that, indeed, they are remaining close to one another.

Baryshnikov often likes to think that he would be happy giving up his public life so he could spend his days at his Hudson River or Connecticut home with his two children, doing a bit of physical labor, "working around the house, going fishing, listening to music," but he fears that lifestyle would not fulfill him.

"Maybe it's an illusion," he says. Close friend Joseph Brodsky says, "By nature [Baryshnikov] is a settler, but his profession makes him a nomad. I think he despises himself for being a dancer. He considers his body a machine, something apart from him."

It must, in part, be the nomad in Baryshnikov that keeps him from making a marriage commitment. Still single, and never before married, the dancer seems to fear his own shortcomings more than those of others. On the subject of marriage, he admits, "I have my hopes, my doubts. Maybe I'm not that kind of person. Maybe I'm too selfish, too demanding, too impatient. I'm not an easy person. I know myself. I'm very moody and unpredictable, but I'm fighting this myself, too. I know my weaknesses; I don't hide them."

Baryshnikov has always been happy to be alone. His moodiness and fundamental unhappiness have caused him to keep many people at a distance throughout his life. He has been reluctant to make lasting attachments—to people or places—and has given up many dear things through the years. He gave up Russia, his family there, his friends there, his career there. He gave up Balanchine, the American Ballet Theatre, and all the people that were a part of those two companies. He gave up Gelsey Kirkland and Jessica Lange. Brodsky says of his friend, "He goes from departure to departure. But he still has the physical capacity to hope, and though he is not cynical, he doesn't expect very much anymore."

One cannot help but think that much of who Baryshnikov is as a person was created by the early loss of his mother. While only eleven years old, Baryshnikov was, in effect, abandoned by the woman who constituted his first permanent attachment. The effects of this event on the psychological development of the dancer cannot be taken lightly. Yet, the same pain that causes his underlying streak of sadness and anger also fuels his emotional depth and his genius. Having experienced the powerful and long-lasting emotions that he has—from the deep sadness of his childhood through the losses caused by his defection—Misha has a constant source to draw upon in his art. He can summon pain and fear on stage with incredible power because he has felt those emotions intensely in his own life. Dance has given Baryshnikov an outlet through which he can express his deepest emotions and can focus his inner-directedness and powerful drive to attain perfection.

A creative person's life, one like Baryshnikov's, is not necessarily a happy one. Misha admits this. "Me? Happy? No. No. There are moments when I'm with my daughter, when we're playing games, and I forget everything and am happy, but in general, I'm not the happiest person in the world." The tremendous urge to create, to produce, and to understand can constantly add tension and turmoil in a creative person's life. Possibilities, says Baryshnikov, keep a person from being content.

> You create problems for yourself; you're solving problems. You think it's possible; you think it's not. Would I do it? Can I do it? No matter how good you feel, there's always the next project, I want to do it first. Will it be fun? Will it not be fun? You're too old to do that; you're not strong enough to do this. You're not talented enough to do this, but that is definitely not your cup of tea. You don't have time; you can't afford it. It's endless. Then you get depressed. I wouldn't know what to do with myself if I was . . . happy.

For the dancer, the price of great achievement in his art has been the incurable sadness in his life.

Is Baryshnikov a genius? The answer is complex. The role of a dancer is very different from that of a writer or a painter. Dancers, like singers and actors, are interpretive artists and, as such, their brilliance often comes with their ability to express works that have been created by others.

In his early years, Baryshnikov's incredible facility with dance enabled him to perform roles with astonishing precision, executing dance steps with textbook technique and achieving extensions and positions with near perfection. In this way, the dancer's early talent was expressed through his control and ability to achieve beauty through effortless grace. For his first eight years, he danced classical roles that had been danced hundreds of times before by other dancers.

As he matured, and his comfort with technique allowed him to focus more on personal interpretation, the dancer set himself apart with his unique portrayals of many standard balletic characters. Baryshnikov also created many roles of his own, dancing parts that were written expressly for him. Later in his career, he put his interpretive stamp on many standard ballets by staging them with his own unique choreography. The new visions of characters and of traditional ballets were Baryshnikov's "creations" as an artist.

Of course, Baryshnikov, like any other dancer, is a product of his teachers and his choreographers. In many ways, the dancer is merely a vehicle, a tool, that is used to express the themes set forth by a director and choreographer. But the expressiveness and versatility of the dancer is what sets him or her apart from others. Many times in the past, as Baryshnikov worked with various choreographers, the dancer's incredible range sparked the creation of new steps, new combinations, new interpretations of a character. In that way, Baryshnikov was indeed a part of the *intellectual* creative process of many new ballets.

Baryshnikov's later career is marked by a noteworthy dedication to apply his classical training to other forms of dance. Through the years, he has performed jazz as well as tap pieces. He has danced and acted in a number of films, on television, and has acted on Broadway with great success. In 1980, he became the artistic director of the American Ballet Theatre in New York. All of these roles have stretched his ability to new limits and have challenged him to continue his growth as an artist.

A dancer's ability to synthesize the ideas of a ballet with the physical execution of its dance is a unique brand of genius—one that Baryshnikov employed without equal. And even though a dancer is primarily a tool through which a dance is expressed, the style and usage of that tool is essentially in the dancer's control. And it is the style and control of the tool that creates the expression of a character on stage. Baryshnikov's exceptional physical range and his expressiveness as an actor enabled him and his choreographers to redefine much of modern ballet in the 1970s and 1980s. His ability to master many different styles of classical ballet and modern dance attest to the thoroughness of his talent. And though his dancing career has by no means come to an end, he has already set a new world standard for the art form of ballet— one that will perhaps never be matched by anyone.

And now, it is time for the dancer to throw himself into a new life. Misha offers his thoughts on his future: "My life has been a bit too crowded, a bit too public. There are certain sides that I now have to explore—in myself as a performer and myself as a man. It's the beginning of my next life. There's nothing planned and nothing prepared. I'm jumping to actually nowhere."

Just as with that unplanned jump he took in Toronto in 1974, Baryshnikov's future is unmapped and unclear. But that uncertainty doesn't seem to bother him, for he knows that whatever he decides to do next, it will pose problems that intrigue him and inspire him. And as he solves those problems, the world will watch him closely, in awe of the man who truly has the courage to jump "to actually nowhere."

CHRONOLOGY

1948   Riga, Latvia, Mikhail is born to Nikolai and
Alexandra Baryshnikov on January 27.

1950   *U.S. troops enter Korea.*

1953   *Stalin dies; U.S. withdraws troops from Korea.*

1956   *Khrushchev denounces Stalin's policies; Soviet
troops march into Hungary.*

1958   *Khrushchev becomes Premier.*

1959   Auditions at the Riga dance school. A few
months later, his mother commits suicide.

1960   Begins his study at the Riga dance school.

1961   *U.S. sends advisors to Vietnam; Berlin Wall is
built.*

1963   *President Kennedy assassinated.*
Invited to join a Riga dance troupe. Tours

Leningrad, meets Alexander Pushkin at the Vaganova School.

1964 *Khrushchev removed from power.*
Accepted to the Vaganova school.

1966 Debut on the Kirov stage, dancing *Le Corsaire* in a student performance from the Vaganova school.

1967 Joins the Kirov company after only three years at Vaganova. Makes his professional debut dancing the Peasant *pas de deux* from *Giselle*.

1968 *USSR invades Czechoslovakia.*

1969 Dances *Romeo and Juliet* with Irina Kolpakova in Igor Tchernichov's production at the Kirov. Later that year, he collaborates on another project with Tchernichov, *Bolero,* and works with Leonid Yakobson on *Vestris.* Dances *Vestris* at the International Ballet Competition in Moscow and wins a gold medal.

1970 Tours London with Kirov. Meets with Rudolf Nureyev and experiences firsthand the realities of defection when Natalia Makarova leaves the troupe and receives political asylum in England. Alexander Pushkin dies of a heart attack.

1971 Plays the toreador in Sergei Yursky's television production of *The Sun Also Rises.* He dances in a made-for-television ballet entitled *The Tale of the Serf Nikishka* under the direction of Kirill Laskari.

1972 Collaborates with two of the Bolshoi's most gifted choreographers, Natalia Kasatkina and Vladimir Vasiliov, on *The Creation of the World.* Debuts as Albrecht in a Kirov production of *Giselle.*

1973 *Peace agreement ends Vietnam War.*
Begins work on a "special evening" that showcases his talent.

1974 *President Nixon resigns over Watergate scandal.*

Meets choreographer Roland Petit in Leningrad. In June, he joins a tour of special dancers that will perform throughout Canada. On June 29, while in Toronto, Baryshnikov defects after a performance of *Don Quixote*. Soon after his defection, Misha performs *La Sylphide* for Canadian television—his first ballet as a non-Russian citizen. A few weeks later, at the request of Natalia Makarova, he joins the American Ballet Theatre (ABT) and makes his New York and American debut in *Giselle*. Begins romantic and professional partnership with Gelsey Kirkland.

1975 An ankle injury during a February performance of *Don Quixote* in Australia leaves the dancer out of commission for five weeks. Collaborates on an innovative production with famed choreographer Roland Petit on *Le Jeune Homme et la Mort*.

1976 Collaborates with celebrated American choreographer Twyla Tharp on *Push Comes to Shove* and explores a different, more modern style of dance. Begins work in Herbert Ross's film about ballet, entitled *The Turning Point*. Makes his debut as a choreographer when his production of *The Nutcracker* premieres at the Kennedy Center in Washington, D.C. in December.

1977 Nominated for an Academy Award as Best Supporting Actor in *The Turning Point*.

1978 Produces *Don Quixote* at the Kennedy Center and receives unfavorable reviews. In the spring, he shocks the ballet world with his announcement that he will leave ABT to dance with George Balanchine's New York City Ballet. Relationship with Gelsey Kirkland ends.

1979 Resigns from the NYCB after his performance of *La Sonnambula* at the Kennedy Center. Begins work on his first American television special, with Liza Minnelli, entitled *Baryshnikov on Broadway*.

1980 *Baryshnikov on Broadway* airs in April and receives mixed reviews. Meets Jessica Lange and begins work as Artistic Director for the ABT.

1981 Alexandra is born to Jessica and Misha.

1982 ABT has one of its most successful seasons in its history. In Chicago, Misha suffers a knee injury during a rehearsal that will keep him off the stage for over six months.

1983 Criticized for not spending enough time with the ABT company, Misha submits his resignation, but it is not accepted.

1984 Mounts a grand new production of *Cinderella* with Peter Anastos that does well at the box office but fails with the critics. Begins work on a Taylor Hackford film project, entitled *White Nights,* in which he co-stars with Gregory Hines and Isabella Rossellini.

1985 *Mikhail Gorbachev assumes power.*
White Nights opens to good reviews and soon becomes a great commercial success at the box office. Jessica and Misha separate for good. Misha becomes more seriously involved with ABT ballerina Lisa Rinehart.

1986 *Perestroika initiated by Gorbachev.*
Works in Italy on a Herbert Ross film entitled *Dancers.* American citizenship is secured.

1987 At age 39, Baryshnikov begins a 35-city tour with ten ballerinas entitled *Baryshnikov and Company,* which sells out across the country. *Dancers* opens in October to disappointing reviews. Misha dances in the highly acclaimed PBS series *Dance in America.*

1988   ABT has its most financially successful season under Baryshnikov's leadership. He choreographs a production of *Swan Lake* and receives serious criticism from dance writers for his direction.

1989   *Massive protests in the Eastern-bloc countries; Berlin Wall comes down.*
Announces his resignation from the ABT. *Metamorphosis* opens on Broadway in May to unfavorable reviews, though Misha's acting is praised by many critics. In July, a son, Peter, is born to Lisa Rinehart and Misha. Announces his resignation from the ABT.

1990   Continues involvement in many marketing and merchandising efforts, including the promotion of his fragrance for women called "Misha" and the creation of his own line of dancewear. He plans to act in a new movie with Gene Hackman and continues to consider new acting roles for Broadway and television. Dances in Mark Morris' company and tours the country with Morris and other dancers.

GLOSSARY

arabesque The extension of one leg straight back, while the position of arms and body may vary.

avant garde Experimental, modern, ahead of its time.

ballon The ability of a dancer to remain suspended in air during a jump; elasticity in jumping.

choreographer Someone who creates a dance.

classical ballet Theatrical dancing in which the basic law is perfect balance. Dances are based on five positions of the feet.

corps de ballet The group members of a dance company.

combination A series of steps that make up a dance or segment of a dance.

danseur noble Leading man in a dance performance.

defection The abandonment of one's country.

demi-caractère A character dancer.

double assemblé Two jumps taken in succession with both feet landing together.

emigré Someone who has immigrated to another country, a new citizen.

expressionistic Exaggerated, jarring, purposely disturbing.

grand jeté A large leap forward.

mentor An influential teacher.

mime The art of portraying a character or of narration by body movements.

pantomime ballet A dance work that makes its points largely through mime gesture related to everyday life rather than through pure dance movement.

pas de deux A dance for two people.

pirouette A turn on one foot propelled by the swing of the arm.

plié A bending of the knees with hips, legs, and feet turned outward and the back held straight.

repertoire The dances a dance company regularly performs.

synthesize To bring parts together and make a whole.

upper echelon The elite in a group of people or an organization.

virtuoso Someone who excels in an artistic endeavor.

BIBLIOGRAPHY

Acocella, Joan Ross. "Double or Nothing: ABT's
Cinderella," *Dance Magazine*. March, 1984, p. 36.

Aloff, Mindy. "American Ballet Theatre's Future: Reflecting on the Anniversary," *Dance Magazine*.
January, 1990, p. 46.

Brubach, Holly. "Lover's Leap: Behind the Scenes
with Baryshnikov," *Vogue*. July, 1987, p. 65.

Baryshnikov, Mikhail. *Baryshnikov*. Charles France,
ed. New York: Abrams, 1980.

"Baryshnikov: Gotta Dance," *Time*. May 19, 1975,
p. 44.

Baryshnikov, Mikhail, and Peter Anastos. *The Swan
Prince*. New York: Bantam, 1987.

Baryshnikov, Mikhail, and Martha Swope. *Baryshnikov
at Work*. New York: Abrams, 1976. (Paperback,
Knopf, 1978.)

Collins, Nancy. "Mikhail Baryshnikov," *Rolling Stone.*
    October 8, 1987, p. 58.

Croce, Arlene. "Midnight," *The New Yorker.* January
    16, 1984, p. 95.

————— "The Search for Cinderella," *The New
    Yorker.* May 21, 1984.

Dalva, Nancy Vreeland. "Baryshnikov's Bug Bit,"
    Dance Magazine. June, 1989, p. 49.

————— "Lisa de Ribere at ABT," *Dance Magazine.*
    May, 1982, p. 45.

Fraser, John. *Private View: Inside Baryshnikov's ABT.*
    New York: Bantam, 1988.

Gruen, John. "Misha of the Muses," *Dance Magazine.*
    October, 1988, p. 68.

Haskell, Molly. "Misha," *Vogue.* November, 1985,
    p. 40.

Horn, Laurie. "Baryshnikov Takes on Swan Lake:
    Something Old, Something New," *Dance Magazine.*
    May, 1989, p. 44.

Horosko, Marian. "Baryshnikov Ignites Steel City,"
    Dance Magazine. April, 1982, p. 52.

Jowitt, Deborah. "Baryshnikov: His Years at ABT,"
    Dance Magazine. January, 1990, p. 38.

Kirkland, Gelsey, and Greg Lawrence. *Dancing on My
    Grave.* New York: Doubleday, 1986.

"Misha in Motion," *Newsweek* ("Newsmakers"). Octo-
    ber 19, 1987.

Saal, Hubert. "Ballet at Its Best," *Newsweek,* May 19,
    1975, p. 62.

Schiff, Stephen. "The Prince Bows Out," *Vanity Fair.*
    November, 1989, p. 188.

Smakov, Gennady. *Baryshnikov: From Russia to the
    West.* New York: Farrar, Straus, & Giroux, 1981.

Stuart, Otis. "ABT at the Met: Big Business," *Dance
    Magazine.* September, 1988, p. 32.

Trustman, Deborah. "Baryshnikov," *The New York
    Times Magazine.* April 11, 1982, p. 27.

INDEX

Photo Credits:

Cover: AP/Wide World Photos; **Cover Insert:** Jack Vartoogian; **Frontispiece,** Pages 56, 69, 72, 81, 84, 86, 94, 100, 102, 106: Martha S wope; 9: Sovfoto; 11, 20: Courtesy of Nina Alovert; 14, 36, 53, 59, 89: AP/Wide World Photos; 17, 38: Patricia Barnes/The Image Works; 25, 28, 31: Tass/Sovfoto; 34, 48: Rosemary Winckley/The Image Works; 42: Novosti/Sovfoto; 45, 61: UPI/Bettmann Newsphotos; 64: Linda Vartoogian; 70: Kobal Collection; 75: Ernst Haas/Magnum Photos; 82, 105: Eve Arnold/Magnum Photos; 96: J.K./Magnum Photos; 108: Reuters/Bettmann Newsphotos. **Color Insert:** Pages 1,8: J. Donoso/Sygma; 2, 4, 6, 7(b): Jack Vartoogian; 3: Kobal Collection; 5: Linda Vartoogian; 7(t):Photofest.

Photo Research: Photosearch, Inc.